D0678493

LOVE CAN BE

JAN -- 2019

LOVE CAN BE

A LITERARY COLLECTION ABOUT OUR ANIMALS

EDITED BY LOUISA McCUNE AND TERESA MILLER

KIRKPATRICK FOUNDATION

Oklahoma City

Copyright © 2018 by Kirkpatrick Foundation

Designed in Oklahoma City. Printed in East Peoria, Illinois.
Published in the United States of America by Kirkpatrick Foundation.

Book design by Christopher Lee
Cover photograph by Joel Sartore
Cover design by Steven Walker
Illustrations by JJ Ritchey

Page 214 constitutes an extension of this copyright page.

This book is a limited edition.

All proceeds benefit six animal charities in Oklahoma;
please refer to page 209 for more information.

First Edition

ISBN 978-0-9996993-0-0

All rights reserved.

Please be kind to animals.

www.kirkpatrickfoundation.com

ABOUT THIS BOOK

Love Can Be is conceived, created, and delivered to readers as a philanthropic endeavor. Creative and printing costs have been incurred by the Kirkpatrick Foundation, so that all net proceeds—less bookseller and distribution fees—will be donated to the designated animal charities. The book is intended as a limited edition.

This book is dedicated to Joan Kirkpatrick,
whose love for animals and generosity made it possible.

TABLE OF CONTENTS

LOUISA McCUNE.. 2
Introduction

URSULA K. LE GUIN 6
The Cat

JULIA ALVAREZ.. 8
Naming the Animals
The Animals Review Pictures of a Vanished Race

BLAKE BAILEY 14
Pretty Girl

RICK BASS 22
Those Who Refuse to Be Chosen

P. C. CAST... 30
My Warrior

WAYNE COYNE.. 40
Frog Patrol and Turtle Dashing

KIM DONER... 44
Rocky Ride

DELIA EPHRON 52
Dogs

REYNA GRANDE 62
A Migrant's Story

JOY HARJO.. 68
Redbird Love
In Honor of Mo Who Is Our Cat, and We Are Hers

AMY HEMPEL 74
   Moonbow

JUAN FELIPE HERRERA 78
   Letter to Sudan: Last White Male Rhino on Earth

S. E. HINTON 82
   Baby Horse

BRANDON HOBSON 92
   Sunlight Travelers

DEAN KOONTZ... 98
   A Spooky Moment Around Which the Entire Story Revolves

JILL McCORKLE 106
   Dogly Prayers and Wishes

TERESA MILLER 114
   The One-Eyed Dog

N. SCOTT MOMADAY 122
   The Bear
   On the Neva

JOYCE CAROL OATES 126
   JUBILATE: An Homage in Catterel Verse

SUSAN ORLEAN 136
   Dog Memory

RON PADGETT 140
   Animals and Art

ELISE PASCHEN 144
   Prey
   Quarrel of Sparrows

DIANE REHM 150
The Emperor Maxie

JEWELL PARKER RHODES 156
Griffin

WADE ROUSE......................................162
Christmas Cookie

ALEXANDER MCCALL SMITH 168
Baboons and Opera

LALITA TADEMY 172
Shadow

CLIFTON TAULBERT 176
Peru and Saturday Afternoon Horses

MICHAEL WALLIS.................................182
Touchstone

MARY LOGAN WOLF 188
Bobcat Magic

ABOUT THE AUTHORS.............................196

KIRKPATRICK FOUNDATION.......................207

HONORARIA 208

BENEFICIARIES 209

ACKNOWLEDGMENTS 212

COPYRIGHTS AND SPECIAL PERMISSIONS 214

LOVE CAN BE

Love can be and sure enough is moving in all things, in all places, in all forms of life at the same snap of your finger.

WOODY GUTHRIE, "My Secret"

INTRODUCTION

T HE EXAMPLES ARE endless. Words and animals have gone together for as long as language has existed. It is among the most natural of creative pairings: animals as subject matter and, in literature, animals as companions to the solitary author.

The most famous writer in modern times to embrace the benefits of animal friends may be Ernest Hemingway, whose polydactyl cats commanded his house in Key West, the descendants of whom now number fifty-four. Mark Twain was also a well-known cat lover: "I simply can't resist a cat, particularly a purring one. They are the cleanest, cunningest, and most intelligent things I know, outside of the girl you love, of course." Twain also articulated the bond that unites people: "When a man loves cats, I am his friend and comrade, without further introduction." T. S. Eliot's *Old Possum's Book of Practical Cats* (1939), the foundation of modern Broadway musicals, was illustrated by the famous book cover artist, Edward Gorey, who summed it up in just five words: "Books. Cats. Life is good." (Upon his death, Gorey left the whole of his estate to animal charities.)

Dogs are similar partners in the creation of literary reputations. John Steinbeck lays claim to the most well-known poodle in modern American letters, Charley, made famous in *Travels with Charley* (1962), in which the aging author and his dog depart their Long Island home, in Sag Harbor, to tour America in a GMC truck with a camper—a vehicle named Rocinante, after Don Quixote's horse. "I've always tried out my material on my dog first," he said.

Kurt Vonnegut, with whom I once spoke on the telephone—a voice gruff from a lifetime of smoking—softened when it came to canines. In *Slapstick* (1976), his free-form, somewhat autobiographical science-fiction novel, he wrote: "I cannot distinguish between the love I have for people and the love I have for dogs." (Vonnegut named his son Mark, after the aforementioned cat lover.)

Charles Dickens was an equal-opportunity animal lover, having his pet, Grip, a favorite black raven, taxidermied and mounted. Southern Gothicist Flannery O'Connor was also a bird lover, known for the peafowl she kept at her Georgia home. In recent years, Jonathan Franzen has become recognized as a first-rate bird-watcher, perhaps as much as he is known for depicting contemporary angst in the middle-American family.

In fact, it's the rare writer—artisan of a craft at times so lonesome as to *require* comrades in sentient life—who hasn't articulated some measure of adoration and advocacy for animals, whether they're inside the house or out. Writing *with* animals seriously aids the hunting and pecking of keyboard strokes, the beloved creatures providing the steady breath of partnership or, more practically, nudging their companions when it's time to be fed, to take a break, to stretch, to pause, or to be let out. Writing *about* animals is an all-consuming exercise in the art of noticing. Watching behavior and turning that observation into words— it's a delightful and sometimes heartbreaking conveyance. *Old Yeller, Beautiful Joe, Charlotte's Web, The Story About Ping*—these are the books of my childhood, robust tales embodied with the highs and lows of life on earth. Animals in literature will touch every emotion, and those in this book do too, from tears to laughter. *Love Can Be* is a celebration of writing with and about animals.

The thirty authors whose works constitute *Love Can Be* were selected for their diversity of perspectives, their connections to the editors, in some cases their connections to Oklahoma, and always their rich viewpoints.

The book was conceived at a meeting in October 2017 at the Oklahoma History Center among me, coeditor Teresa Miller, and Oklahoma historian Bob Blackburn. It was first thought of as a possible companion publication to a photographic exhibition about animals in Oklahoma history, but the projects quickly became separate endeavors, each having its own creative scope and course. Their respective titles, however, are connected, and linked to great Oklahomans: *Love Can Be,* from a piece of Woody Guthrie prose, and *Where They Went*, an homage to a quote attributed to Will Rogers, "If there are no dogs in Heaven, then when I die I want to go where they went."

Strictly by the numbers, our thirty authors have a wide spectrum of achievements. They are the recipients of dozens, if not hundreds, of awards, including the National Medal of Arts, the Guggenheim Fellowship, the National Book Critics Circle Award, the Pulitzer Prize, the Grammy Award, the American Book Award, the Wallace Stevens Award, the National Book Award, the Personal Peabody Award, the National Humanities Medal, the PEN/Malamud Award for Short Fiction, and more. In the end, awards mean little, but they do tell a story of talent, tenacity, and a bit of luck. We are honored and excited to include each of these writers here.

Eighteen pieces in the book are original, and twelve are reprints. Likewise, eighteen authors are women; twelve are men. Six pieces are about cats, ten about dogs, two about horses, and two about butterflies. We have an elegy for the last white male rhino, a meditation about a bobcat roaming through eastern Oklahoma County, and twenty bears in Montana needing protection. The rest of the essays are a beautiful, comprehensive menagerie.

At Kirkpatrick Foundation, the impetus for this book—and for all of our animal-related endeavors—is to educate and inspire the public to value animal wellbeing in their own lives and communities. In 2012, the foundation debuted its initiative Safe & Humane, to make Oklahoma the safest and most humane place to be an animal by the year 2032. It's an admittedly ambitious goal and one we work on every day in some capacity. The scope of the foundation's work includes grant-making, convening, research, recognition, and, as here, publishing. *Love Can Be* adds to our existing suite of publications and is the first to embrace the literary arts in a way that supports animal charities through traditional book sales.

As I write this, my mother's cat, Dark Shadow, my newest feline since her recent death, is standing on his hind legs with his paws in my lap, endeavoring to interrupt a morning's progress. At my house, three sons, five cats, and two dogs—eleven of us in total—combine for lively days and settled nights, our bedsides shared with a mix of species. A sleeping cat atop my desk is a sure sign that all is well. So too, as for many writers, is a dog snoring and asleep at my feet. (Writes Vonnegut in *Slaughterhouse-Five*: "And the dog of my future, lying at my feet, is snoring now.")

Of all the people involved in the making of this book, there is one without whom it simply would not exist. Joan Kirkpatrick was ahead of her time, an Oklahoma animal advocate long before the rise of local humane groups and the movement to protect animals globally. The daughter of Kirkpatrick Foundation founders John and Eleanor Kirkpatrick, she led the foundation's early animal-welfare activities with the advancement of veterinary sciences and rescue funding. When Joan died in 2009, she left a portion of her estate to the Kirkpatrick Foundation for the benefit of animals. With her spirit and values as guiding principles, we dedicate this book to her.

LOUISA McCUNE

Oklahoma City, August 2018

MOE BOWSTERN

*Ursula K. Le Guin (1929–2018) works alongside Pard,
who makes himself comfortable among notes and trinkets
atop the "Time Machine"—one of many Pard-isms
found in Le Guin's blog,* The Annals of Pard.

The Cat

URSULA K. LE GUIN

He walks upon his paws
To the places that he goes,
Followed by his tail
And preceded by his nose.

He knows what he is doing.
He goes about his business.
He need not explain it.
He is being his isness.

*Julia Alvarez feeding chickens on the eleven-acre farm
in Vermont where she and her husband, Bill Eichner,
once lived with a menagerie of farm animals*

© BILL EICHNER

Naming the Animals

JULIA ALVAREZ

Let's name the animals no longer with us,
except in language: start with the dodo,
the Haitian long-tongued bat, the dwarf emu,
the laughing owl, the eastern buffalo.
And then animals like the nukupuu,
the lorikeet, the broad-faced potoroo,
whose absences don't sadden me as much
as I can't put a picture to their names:
two potoroos, say, lounging in their den
with baby potoroos clambering over them.

I think of Adam watching the parade
of just-created animals, their form
still taking shape, so had he touched too hard,
the camel might have had some extra humps,
the colors might have smudged on the peacock,
which wasn't yet a peacock, but a thing,
a brightly colored, gorgeous, feathered thing
in need of a name—as was the camel,
the marmoset, the deer, the parakeet,
waiting to enter language and be claimed.

But now, we, Adam's babies, find ourselves
uttering names no one comes up to claim:
no iridescent, billed, web-footed thing
quacks back when we say *Leguat's gelinote*—
in fact, unless we say the name out loud
or write it down, the gelinote is gone.
And so, our language, which singles us out
from dwarf emus, nukupuus, potoroos,
becomes an elegy, as with each loss
our humanness begins to vanish, too.

The Animals Review Pictures of a Vanished Race

"Look at this most curious specimen!"
the cricket chirps, holding a photograph
of a line of chorus girls in bathing suits
kicking their legs. "I think it's more than one,"
the centipede points out. "But yes, they're odd."
"Wait till you see the markings on this one!"
the bulldog growls, tossing a black and white
of a chain gang digging in their prison stripes.
"No kin to us!" the outraged zebras shout.
"Observe the evil flatness of their snouts."

Foxes, flies, penguins, ladybugs, lions—
in short, the whole animal kingdom has come
to celebrate the lucky extinction
of Earth's worst enemy and take a vote
on whether to elect a new top dog.
"Cease from using species-specific terms!"
the snakes protest. Of course, they're sensitive,
maligned for generations as the cause
of mankind's fall. Meanwhile, as next of kin,
the chimps keep bringing up the missing link.

After a *No!* vote, the animals pile up
the memorabilia of the vanished race—
pictures of kings, ice-skaters, terrorists—
then light the pyre. Not a trace remains
of those who poisoned, ravaged, and exploited
their common home—or almost none remain.
A love-struck chimp has sneaked a picture out,
torn from the frontispiece of a book of poems,
and hidden inside a banana peel,
of (possibly?) Emily Dickinson.

Blake Bailey and his beagle Polly watch an eclipse near the water's edge in Portsmouth, Virginia.

Pretty Girl

BLAKE BAILEY

THAT WAS THE year we moved to the town of Waldo, Florida, a notorious speed trap about thirteen miles northeast of Gainesville, where my wife was a graduate student (psychology) at the university. The idea was to get away from the seedy student apartment complex— all we could afford at the time—where our neighbors liked to lounge in their cars listening to stereos that sounded like depth bombs exploding beneath the window where I sat trying to write a book. In Waldo we lived a block from the train tracks, a feature we hadn't noticed when we decided to rent the little concrete bungalow with a screen porch and kumquat tree in the yard. Between us and the racket of passing boxcars were four derelict trailer houses, which were vacant at first, then occupied by rustic meth-heads who, we learned, were all cousins or in any case vaguely related.

The nearest meth-head was Butch, a ropey guy with a scraggly goatee whose yard was divided from ours by a sagging metal fence. Butch had a small daughter (where is she now?) who'd stand there, wanly dazed, whenever Butch's ex-wife would drop her off and remind Butch, in passing, of his various shortcomings.

"What about *yew?*" Butch would riposte. "Yer a *whore!*"

The woman would laugh, bitterly, and taunt Butch about all the men—better men than he, she was careful to note—she'd recently "been with." The little girl stood there. We sat at a distance watching from our screen porch, a sort of fourth wall that sequestered us from

the tempest. Also among the observers was a big black dog Butch kept
in his yard on a twenty-foot chain. The dog was a mystery. I rarely saw
Butch acknowledge her in any way, and the small daughter seemed too
bewildered to notice her either. The dog didn't seem to mind: During
these operatic disputes between Butch and his ex-wife, the dog would
stand there wagging her tail in a kind of tentative, hopeful way.

We got the idea the trailer people were somehow related on the
day Butch overdosed that first time. A gaunt woman and her two
children, subjects for a Walker Evans photo, came over from one of
the other trailers and paced along our common fence, joined every so
often in furtive parley by one or two of her neighbors, who vaguely
resembled her. The dog walked among them, as far to either side as
her chain would permit. The gaunt woman's kids also ignored the dog.
Eventually an ambulance arrived and shambled to a halt in Butch's
rutted yard, its lights flashing topsy-turvy in the evening twilight.
The gaunt woman watched, grimly smoking, while medics entered
the trailer and emerged with Butch loaded on a gurney, gaping like a
bludgeoned catfish.

"Um, is he gonna be OK?" I asked the woman.

Sucking her cigarette between thumb and forefinger, she said
something about Butch never having no damn sense no how. Even
when they was kids. She sighed and watched the ambulance leave, then
wandered back to her own trailer while her children straggled behind
her as if on a generous length of string. Boxcars rattled in the distance.

Butch was gone for a few wet autumn days. The black dog didn't
seem to mind at first, frisking about on her chain, but gradually she
seemed to wind down and move less and less until finally she just
sat there in the chilly drizzle. There was no shelter, nor did Butch's
cousins in the other trailers show any interest. Finally I grabbed a

bag of cat food (we had a cat and would occasionally feed other cats who wandered over, unfed, from the nearby trailers) and went out in the rain to feed Butch's dog.

When I got close, I saw the dog's chain was snarled into a tight ball and coated in a stew of mud and feces from where the dog was forced to sit. I proffered a bowl of cat food and she took a few bites, more to oblige me than because she was still capable of hunger. Rather than let her off the chain to run free and take her own chances at a better life, I phoned animal control and they promptly came and took her away. A notice was posted on Butch's door informing him that he had X days to post a fine and collect his dog, or else she'd be euthanized.

"I hope he doesn't shoot us," my wife said.

"Maybe he'll think one of the cousins did it?"

"Right."

The next day or two Butch came back, looking paler and a little stooped but not terribly worse for wear. To our surprise he paid the fine and brought his dog back, then proceeded to build a kind of ramshackle shelter out of wood scraps and chicken wire; presumably he'd been told at animal control that he had to do better than a chain per se. If he bore us any animus for ratting him out, he didn't let on, but then he and his cousins were inscrutable that way.

The dog lost no time escaping. I was reading on my porch when it happened. I lowered my book to watch the dog's frenzied digging, the way she paused now and then to sniff the air and make sure the coast was clear. Finally she shimmied under the wire, shook off the excess dirt, and barrel-assed up the gravel road toward the highway. We never saw her again. I imagine she got hit by a car or a train or maybe picked up again by animal control and put down.

Butch, for his part, did not observe a seemly mourning period.

"Purty Girl Purty Girl Purty Girl!" we heard him yodeling a few days later. Pretty Girl was a white pit bull puppy with darkish spots under her coat suggesting a hint of Dalmatian in her lineage. She gamboled at Butch's feet, then darted off in blurry circles around his trailer while he gave staggering, laughing pursuit. A few of his cousins wandered over to join the fun. In fifteen minutes the puppy had gotten more attention than her predecessor in as many months.

"Enjoy it while you can," I thought. By then we'd figured out why we were feeding so many cats, and never mind the starving black dog on her filthy chain: Butch and his cousins loved pets as kittens and puppies, then lost interest as they got big and hungry and less cute.

But Pretty Girl seemed to have their number. One morning we heard a rapping on our bedroom window, followed by the ambient sizzle of a small but fleet dog zooming amid the dead leaves around our house. Every few seconds a white streak would appear in our bedroom window, and finally we heard a polite, panting *woof-woof* outside the screened porch. "Can you spare some food?" she was asking, in effect, and we gave her a bowl of cat chow.

This became a morning routine. She'd take a stick in her mouth and knock or drag it against our window (nobody believes that part), then run around the house until hunger got the best of her. The weird part was this: After bolting her cat food, and accepting a little heartfelt petting and cooing, she'd go right back to her crappy dog run chez Butch. She liked him, whether he bothered to feed her or not.

Within a few days we'd given her a different name, Puppasaurus, and taken other propriety measures such as buying her a leash and collar and taking her for quick, nervous walks whenever Butch's truck wasn't around. The dog liked exploring the countryside on her own, too, and sometimes she'd appear out of nowhere during my afternoon jog, adjusting her pace to mine and all but waving me on whenever she had to stop for a dump—a solemn, dilatory business—whereupon she'd race back to my side and resume her obliging trot. One time Butch rattled by in his truck and I expected a dirty look, but not at all: *"Purty Girl Purty Girl Purty Girl!"* he yodeled out his window, and she promptly abandoned me to chase him back home.

One evening I went outside and found a familiar scene: an ambulance parked in Butch's yard, a few of the cousins dappled in the flashing lights, and Puppasaurus sniffing the gurney as it came out of the trailer bearing her comatose master. A few minutes later the ambulance wobbled back to the road and wailed off into the night, a white pit bull loping in its wake like a porpoise.

A week passed, and no Puppasaurus. Given the black dog's vanishing, we feared the worst and were surprised by how bereft we felt. She'd become more than a kind of novel alarm clock; she was almost the naughty daughter we'd yet to have (but would, someday, when we were less busy and poor), a daughter who inexplicably preferred a peckerwood meth-head who rarely bothered to feed her.

Animal control was just off Waldo Road on the way to Gainesville, and the next day my wife paid a visit on her way home from campus. Sure enough Puppasaurus was in one of the little cages and greeted my wife with a big panting smile as if she'd known all along she was too young and comely to suffer the fate of her fellow inmates. In fact she was a day or two away from extinction, and my wife adopted her on the spot.

"Purty Girl Purty Girl Purty Girl!" I yodeled à la Butch when I saw them drive up, and the dog bounded out of the car and splattered herself against our porch screen.

"From now on," my wife said, "her name is Puppasaurus."

Of course we worried what Butch would do when he found out

we'd adopted his dog, and somewhat hoped his latest mishap had resulted in, if not death, at least long-term rehab. But no. One day he came back—the very day we installed Puppasaurus in a spacious Walmart dog pen out by the kumquat tree, a few steps from the porch where I sat pretending to read as Butch pulled into his driveway, saw what he saw, and walked slowly over to my side of the fence.

"Hey, Butch!" I said. "You're back!"

"Yew done trubbled me fer the last time, bwah," I expected him to say, in effect, but he didn't. Rather he said, "I appreciate y'all takin' care of Purty Girl. Guess I caint afford no dog right now, with one thing and another. Glad she got herself a good home." He blew a kiss to Pretty Girl in her pen, and she gave him a brief, ambivalent wag of her tail.

"Feel free to visit her," I said. "We just, you know, Butch, we just didn't want her to get put down."

"I know that. I do."

He nodded dolefully at his feet, but really he seemed relieved he wouldn't have to worry about feeding the dog or feeling guilty about not feeding her. Nor did he ever accept my invitation to visit, though sometimes he'd yodel *Purty Girl Purty Girl Purty Girl!* when he saw us returning from a walk or jog, and I always made a point of letting her off her leash. Away she'd go, bang, hastening to the duty (as perhaps she saw it) of licking this dirty man's beard, but always she returned just as happily, within thirty seconds or so, to the people who not only loved her—as Butch did, after his fashion—but would feed her for many years thereafter.

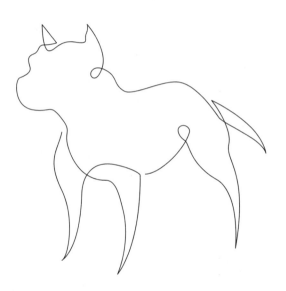

JESSIE GROSSMAN

Rick Bass with Linus (left), a French Brittany, and Callie, a German Shorthaired Pointer. According to Rick's memoir, The Traveling Feast, *the dogs often accompany him on his road trips.*

Those Who Refuse to Be Chosen

RICK BASS

WE APPLY SO much attention and so many resources to enhancing the lives of the domestic, the animals we have chosen to spend their lives with us as we stumble our way along on the journey that Darwin termed "descent, with modifications." We are so young in the world—depending upon whether one is a lumper or a splitter, somewhere around 180,000 years old. An eyeblink, compared to the length of time that almost all other animals have been in the world. Little wonder, then, that one of our first acts of survival, as we modified into an upright, thinking (presumably) species, hiding out from the swirling harshness of the beautiful world into which we fell, blinking, was to reach back toward the main trunk of the tree of life and grasp for the strength and assurance of wild things.

To domesticate the wolves, to domesticate the wild horses and the birds we liked to eat, even as we edged farther away from that tree's trunk, creeping out on a branch that did not yet sag under the weight of our experimentation—nor had we yet edged out so far that we felt and then knew a terrible estrangement and loneliness—though of course one day that branch would bow and even begin to make splintering sounds, as disturbing as the crack of ice beneath one's feet, were one to venture out onto a sheet of thinning ice so late, too late, in the spring.

And one day the first cold breath of the end of things would begin to be heard—a whisper, at first, the breath of a loneliness so complete that it was understood not to be the end, but the end of the end with no longer any of the second chances and hopes that used to be fuel for the burning condition of life. "Lord, let me die but not die out," writes the poet James Dickey in "For the Last Wolverine."

The wild ones we reached back for—took from the center of the tree's trunk, to carry with us—were and are doomed, then, to accompany their masters on their masters' journey into loneliness, and into the space, the void, that lies beyond the tree. Following us, they renounced their allegiance to where they had lived and what they once were, and were made more tame by us—generation by generation, as if we were little gods.

We fed them, watered them, selecting them for those who would love us most, or what we viewed as most, which is to say unconditionally. We asked them to join us on this journey away from the trunk and—whether willing or unwilling, at first—they followed. They became more adorable. We trained them—bred them—to see what we thought of as our best selves, and bred them evermore toward what we thought was interesting, or beautiful.

Seemingly uncorrupted any longer by the messy calculus of the need to hunt and kill for their sustenance—to be nurtured and fed instead by a master—these once-wild and now-domesticated animals have become ever more adorable, and ever more dependent upon us for their health and well-being.

I'm not pure in this matter. My own pets—a French Brittany named Linus and a German Shorthaired Pointer named Callie—help me find upland game birds (Hungarian partridges and ring-necked pheasants) which I feed upon, even as I feed Callie and Linus.

I did not name Linus. I favored Lucky Ned Pepper but was outvoted.

It's somewhat chastening to be striding the prairie, gun in hand, and, when the pup runs off—or, for that matter, at the urban dog park—to find one's self shouting the word "Linus!" to the sky. The only name I can think of with more baggage in this regard is "Superman"— at the time, the sweetest pointer I had ever owned.

Why are the ones with the silliest names the biggest runners?

I digress, and at a time when the earth is burning, and I do not mean figuratively.

It can be argued, and accurately, I think, that it is when one is at war that digression, distraction, and entertainment can be a valuable form of coping—a survival mechanism. To live in the adrenalized state of constant crisis is no life at all, but instead mere imprisonment.

There is a huge need, then—an immense responsibility—for us to reform our relationships with the wild ones who were left behind, whom we did not choose, or who refused to be chosen, refused to be tamed. Are they not the gold standard of the way we all once were, in the garden, the first garden, from which everything else—the weak and the strong—has come?

Rhinos, gorillas, elephants, gazelles, humpback whales, grizzly bears—this world was once not too small for anyone, was not too small for any creature's dream of life, whether meek or strong. That we have gone out on a limb may be our destiny, and that we took with us some emissaries from that central trunk—but what sense does it make, in our continued leave-taking, to turn back and strike and hew with sharpest axes the very tree from which we originated? One would think self-interest would prevail—what good are the branches if the trunk is damaged, and how long before the branches themselves then weaken and wither? And even if one did not recognize the self-interest in protecting the trunk, the first garden—if, say, one is not able to understand the science of this—then would not simple good manners suffice?

I do not mean to represent myself as a paragon of manners—indeed, my two conditions of being seem to vacillate between socially inattentive / clueless to general pissed-offedness. So when I say that I have spent thirty-plus years fighting for a million acres of public land in northwestern Montana, one million acres of breathtaking jungle diversity—swamps and creeks, and low rounded mountains—and yet have not succeeded in seeing a single acre of it protected, understand there is some self-interest involved. I love to ramble these mountains, to bushwhack through the dense forest, to hunt, occasionally, not as a drive-by shooter cruising a logging road and taking an animal as if with no more skill or respect (much less reverence) than operating a toggle switch or joystick—but to instead travel as far back into the last fourteen pockets of roadless areas in this valley, the Yaak Valley, up on the US–Canada border, as well as the Idaho–Montana border, where the wildest things can still sometimes be found.

As I said, I've been doing it for over thirty years. I have not used up any of the good country, in my quiet and singular walks, but I have used up a good bit of myself. I'm not sure how much more tread I have left—knees, hips, ankles, the whole fragile, fraying mechanism. But I do keep working. I work harder than ever. It seems unfair for me to have had this experience and yet for others to not. The walking, and the working.

There are 640 million acres of public land in the United States. There are roughly 107 million acres of National Forest lands that qualify as "roadless"—gardens of ecological integrity greater than

5,000 acres in size. These last areas are the source of nearly a quarter of our country's freshwater—our own species' most vital and pressing survival need, now and evermore into the future—and are also in many cases the last refuge for our country's woefully lengthening list of threatened, endangered, and sensitive species. There are many in our country who still believe it is not just our pleasure but our responsibility to help protect these time-crafted wonders—animals such as the lynx, wolf, wolverine, woodland caribou, and, most dramatic among them all, the grizzly bear.

Religious philosophers have used words like *stewardship*, with respect to our relationship to all animals and all the earth, and even each other—loving and doing for others as one would one's self—and that's fine by me. In theory, I only wish I could see what stewardship—real stewardship, at a national scale, across all our public lands—looked like in practice.

There is constant corporate pressure to clear-cut timber and dig ore from these last roadless lands, to build steep roads up into the last of them, rather than preserving them for all time as wilderness—free to grow old, rot or burn, and start over, in the cycle of nature and its longer, larger integrity, where these rarest species, time-crafted, still cling. And most dangerous of all, in this day and age, is the heated breath of industrial recreation that is being focused on these last and fragile places: mountain bikes, motorbikes, trail runners, thru-hikers, endurance jocks with stopwatches, all weaving a noisome and stinking thousand-fold or two-thousand-fold presence through the stronghold, the last border refuge, of my valley's last twenty grizzly bears.

No one sets out on a trail with the intent of stressing grizzly bears. What harm can one person do? What is dangerous—for thru-hikers as well as bears—is when the numbers begin to stack up.

A group I'm involved with, the Yaak Valley Forest Council, is supporting—along with a lot of other people—a scenic route that detours around the garden where the Yaak's last twenty grizzlies are holding on, trying to survive, trying to not get in trouble, trying to continue going about the business of just being bears in the high country. Extinction is not the bears' choice. Their beauty has been crafted hard to an extraordinary place; having achieved and attained it—why should they now be crushed, vandalized, erased? If I sound angry, it's because I am. Twenty are not enough.

PUBLISHER'S NOTE: To learn more about the grizzly bears of Yaak Valley, please visit yaakvalley.org.

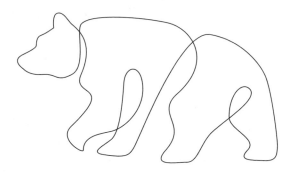

P. C. Cast and Badger have a unique bond—as a specially trained protection dog, Badger is always working. His skills inspired Moon Chosen, *the first book in Cast's series* Tales of a New World.

DANIEL STARK, STARK PHOTOGRAPHY

My Warrior

P. C. CAST

MY STORY WITH Badger begins in 2012, when an unstable young woman fixated on me to the point of becoming a stalker. I was happily living in midtown Tulsa in a lovely little cottage that had close to zero security. Why would I have needed security? Until 2009, when my eighteenth published book debuted at the No. 2 spot on the *New York Times* best-seller list, I'd been a struggling Broken Arrow public school teacher from a family of teachers—who happened to write in her "spare" time. I didn't have much more to "secure" than a negative balance in my checking account and some boxed wine in the fridge. Then the *House of Night* burst onto the best-seller lists, changing my life—but not so much changing *me*. I was perfectly content living in my little midtown cottage and sitting on my front porch with a cold drink, mosquito repellent, and a large fan.

People like to talk about how success changes things. Sadly, those changes can often make the person who experiences the success a target—a lesson my stalker taught me. I tried to ignore her. I didn't publicly bad-mouth her or shame her for her instability and delusions. But I did hire a security team to evaluate exactly how much danger I was in. In just one day—one short afternoon—the security team logged that she had passed my home *thirty-eight times* (driving erratically), and that was a slow stalker day.

I'd lived in the Tulsa area a long time, and I was easy to find. I love midtown and often enjoy its many wonderful restaurants (Wild

Fork! Palace Café! Lucky's!). Utica Square is a favorite haunt of mine. I belonged to the same gym for years (Fit For Her on Brookside!). I had the same hair salon (Ilhoff!) for years as well. I shopped at the Whole Foods on Forty-First Street. I was predictable, which my stalker proved by showing up at these places regularly to attempt to intimidate and hassle me.

I stopped going out. I withdrew. It made me unimaginably angry! I vowed not to allow one unhinged person to dictate my day-to-day activities. But my choices were limited. Restraining orders really work only in retrospect. It seemed ridiculous to me to consider having a security guard with me whenever I left my house, though I did have guards watching my home and added cameras and a security system as well. But as time went on I realized that I was truly in danger, so I paid attention when a good friend recommended I look into getting a personal-protection canine.

I'm definitely an animal person. I was raised with horses, dogs, goats, cats, rabbits, guinea pigs, and even a pheasant chick I tried (unsuccessfully) to rescue and raise. So the thought of having a dog that had been trained specifically to protect me and accompany me during my daily routine initially sounded pretty awesome, but I did have some trepidation. I already had several cats and two Scottie dogs. Would another dog fit in with my pack? I understood that he would be a "working canine," but did that mean he was like a machine? Would he love me? Would he have any personality at all? Would he get along with my friends and family?

As I researched personal-protection canines, I learned that the majority of them are either German shepherds or Belgian Malinois. I knew nothing about either breed. The more research I did, the more I realized how much I didn't know, but I've never been afraid of learning and trying new things—so I agreed to purchase a working canine from a protection-dog agency on the East Coast.

It was a complex process. The protection-dog agency did a lengthy interview with me because they provide canines that are specifically trained for individual situations. They needed to understand my daily habits, how my household ran, etc., so they could pair me with the perfect canine. Finally, they sent me pictures and videos of prospective protection canines. I was drawn to the German shepherds. This agency acquired only East European German shepherds, which have a body type that is different from the black-and-tan, slope-backed dogs most Americans are familiar with. East European shepherds have larger bodies, wider and deeper chests, bigger heads, and different coloring.

My choices were narrowed down until I finally said yes to one particular dog. His name was Odin, though he never knew it. He had been trained not to respond to his name so that bad guys couldn't call him away from his handler. After I said yes to him, I was sent a list of his commands—most of which were in German, though to date he responds to commands in four languages. The list further intimidated me and reminded me that I was getting a dog that had been trained to attack bad guys—*and I was going to have to learn to handle him!*

It was a sweltering triple-digit Oklahoma summer day when Odin arrived in Tulsa—delivered by his trainer and a decoy. Decoy! That's what they call the grown man who puts on a bite suit and lets a 100-plus-pound dog attack him.

I'll never forget meeting my warrior for the first time. He was in a super-sized crate in the back of an SUV. I'd been warned, "Odin's a big boy." I'd assured everyone involved that big dogs do not intimidate me—I like them. So, with confidence, I went to the SUV. The trainer opened his crate and let him out. I distinctly remember my first two thoughts:

(1) *Wow, he is big!* And (2) *Oh, man, I hope he doesn't mind if I play with those huge fluffy ears of his!*

He looked at me. I stared at him—not understanding then that staring into the eyes of any dog, but most especially a trained protection canine, is a sign of aggression. But instead of giving me what we've come to affectionately call his "crazy bug-eyed look," it was love at first sight. From the moment we met, I felt connected to him. It's difficult to explain because it all happened nonverbally. It was a *feeling* I had, and still have—like we were meant to be together—that he was meant to be my protector, that I would never have to worry about my safety as long as he was by my side.

We began training together immediately. I had a lot to learn in the four days allotted to us. We started with basic obedience. When I was a little girl, I'd taken our family basset hound through a 4-H class on dog obedience. Well, let me tell you, that was *nothing* like learning obedience with a working dog. Most of his commands were not in English, even for simple things like sit, down, and heel. But I'm a fast learner, especially when I'm in love—and I was definitely falling in love.

Odin was perfect. He moved with me like we were dancing. The trainer, whom I'll call Jeff, had me take Odin through what was basically an obedience confidence course, and at the end of it, after he and I came to a stop in front of Jeff, he declared, *"Wow! Perfect!"* At that moment I acted on instinct. I threw my arms around Odin's neck and kissed the top of his head.

From the corner of my eye I saw Jeff and the decoy *cringe*—like they expected something awful to happen. But Odin just sat there, wagging his tail and giving me a tongue-lolling doggie grin. Yet his trainer and decoy were acting like he was a bomb waiting to explode all over me. It was then that I realized this dog had more of a story to tell than they were admitting.

That evening, within twenty-four hours of Odin being delivered, we were walking down the sidewalk in front of the Campbell Hotel on Eleventh Street. Odin was off-leash beside Jeff, who was in front of me. I was already so bonded to Odin that I was irritated he was walking with Jeff, so I said, *"Fuss!"* (pronounced *foos*), which is his command to heel. Odin spun around and came instantly to my side. Jeff said in the decades he'd been training and delivering canines, he'd rarely had a new owner call a dog away from him, especially not so soon.

The next day Odin and I did our first bite work together. I'll admit to being very nervous. I wasn't nervous about Odin—he was perfect. I was worried that I would mess up and confuse him. I already wanted to be as perfect for him as he was for me. And, truthfully, I had no real interest in bite work. It was enough for me to know that he had been trained as a weapon, and that he would protect me. The "attack" part of my attack dog was something I didn't even like to think about, let alone practice.

But practice we did!

I was shocked to learn how much fun it was! I give all the credit to Odin. He was spectacular—patient, smart, and increasingly affectionate with me. He taught me to trust that he had my back— literally and figuratively. It is definitely an adrenaline rush to control this huge biting machine.

I've loved many dogs, but I've never had a connection with one like I have with Odin. It's not just his intelligence and size. It's his very being. He exudes strength and confidence and, with me, love. I adored my big warrior, but as Paul Harvey used to say, I also wanted *the rest of the story*. So, before Jeff and the decoy returned to the East

Coast, I plied them with alcohol and learned Odin's story. He'd been born in Czechoslovakia and had just turned five years old. He was a European Schutzhund champion (a dog sport that involves obedience, scent work, and bite work), and had been recruited from the dog-sport arena for personal protection. He'd been sold to a Middle Eastern princess but returned, because he hadn't been trained to heel alongside her horses (I have horses and he heels just fine beside them). Then he'd been sold to a very macho American movie star, who also returned him because Odin had been too aggressive.

I learned those stories as Odin was sprawled out on his side with his head in my lap while I sat on the floor and brushed him. Jeff and the decoy just kept staring at Odin and me as if we were aliens, and as I groomed him and found matted fur under the top layer of his thick, beautiful coat, I realized I was probably the first person in his life to treat him like he was more than a weapon.

Jeff and the decoy left after giving me the instruction that I must have Odin attached to me for thirty solid days—literally every waking moment—so that we would continue to bond. They also left me with thick pinch collars and a shock collar with a remote control, which I *must* keep on him anytime he wasn't in his crate—implying that I would not be able to control him without it. Then Jeff did a lot of bragging about how he was beginning to train "naked" protection dogs, which means training without force (shock collars, pinch collars, etc.), but that I shouldn't try that because a canine like Odin really had to be "broken" first, and only then could he be trusted to obey without force.

Odin and I prove Jeff wrong every day. Yes, I kept Odin attached to me, literally, for thirty days—and for an entire year after that I went nowhere he couldn't go, too. He became part of my pack—and part of my family. Jeff also warned that working dogs, especially aggressive males like Odin, had to be watched around other dogs because they'd spent their lives segregated from them—the reasoning being that they were too aggressive to be part of a pack. Odin proved Jeff wrong about that, too. Besides me, his greatest love is for other dogs and cats—especially puppies! At this moment he is curled up next to me in his big bed with three sleeping Scottie dogs, and just a few minutes ago, when he got up to get a drink, he had to go check on my Maine coon, who licked his nose and rubbed her face all over his.

I changed his name. As I mentioned earlier, he didn't realize he was "Odin" anyway. My family and I now call him Badger, or Badge. And he definitely knows who he is and where he belongs. Good luck to anyone who tries to call him away from me; that will never happen.

It didn't take me long to find the keloids under the thick fur around his neck, from being treated roughly with a pinch collar. I also found wounds and scars from the metal contact points on his electric collar. Recently, almost six years after he entered my life, he injured his back, and I had a series of X-rays done, which revealed old rib fractures. You'll forgive me if I sound violent, but I would like to find those men who "trained" Badge with such horrible force and see how much they like being kicked in the ribs, choked out, and shocked.

But Badge's days of being treated like a soulless weapon are over forever. Instead of shocking him, I use my voice or a clicker, or simply his favorite ball (as a reward), and he performs for me with enthusiasm, intelligence, and love. I have no doubt that Badger would give his life to protect me—without being shocked or choked.

Which brings me to something Badger helped me to discover. As a woman I have, for my entire life, had to be cognizant of possible danger. Like most women, I always park under a street lamp. I have my keys out when I approach my vehicle. I have a concealed carry license. I don't walk down dark streets alone. Being a female in America means that I have to be hypervigilant, and even then I am still nervous about parking garages, walking to my car alone, talking to male strangers, etc.

Enter Badger—my 112.7-pound personal-protection canine, who looks like a grizzly bear and who is *always* on guard. The first time it happened I was so shocked by the feeling that I remember laughing with joy. I was meeting a friend in downtown Tulsa for dinner at Yokozuna Sushi, one of my favorite restaurants. The best place to park is across the street in a rather dark parking lot, but that night it was especially busy, and I drove around and around, trying to find an open spot under a street lamp. Then it hit me—*I had Badger!* Gleefully, I parked in the *back of the lot,* where there was little light and a lot of open spots.

I opened the car door and Badge was immediately at my side— head up, ears pricked, tail up, ever vigilant. For the first time in my adult life I felt safe—really safe—walking alone at night in the dark. And I realized that this must be how men, especially white men, feel all the time! Wow! What a sense of freedom! What a lack of stress! Were there men in that dark parking lot as I walked through it with Badger by my side? Yes. Did they look at me? Absolutely. Did they catcall? Did they approach me? Did I feel threatened by them? ABSOLUTELY NOT.

A good friend of mine analogized that Badger had turned me into the only girl on the playground who had a baseball bat—and was not afraid to use it. At first I laughed and thought it was a funny comparison. But it really isn't, is it? The true analogy is that I was a girl who, for the first time in her adult life, felt immune to the intimidation and abuse that women in this country face daily. I will be forever grateful to Badger for allowing me to feel that beautiful sense of freedom.

Badger is now almost eleven years old. Because he was trained so roughly for the first five years of his life, he has been diagnosed with degenerative disc disease, and now it is my turn to take care of my warrior and be sure he moves gracefully through his senior years. My debt to him is one of commitment, appreciation, and unconditional love, and my wish for the future is that someday in our great country everyone—no matter their sex, race, or gender preference—will be able to walk down the street with the sense of freedom and security my warrior has given me.

GEORGE SALISBURY

*Wayne Coyne with a photo of his younger self
from his frog-catching days*

Frog Patrol and Turtle Dashing

WAYNE COYNE

SUMMERS IN OKLAHOMA (if you live here you already know this) can be *nice,* can be *hot,* and can be fatiguingly *hot* ... oh ... and humid, too. So, yeah, sweaty. On a summer night, it can still be eighty degrees even at two o'clock in the morning. I actually think seventy-seven degrees with no wind is the perfect condition for being naked outside, but that's a different story. This story is from when I was very young, eight or nine years old. We would wear jeans and be barefoot. So, the daytime would be insanely hot. Too hot to do anything outside. But the nights would be perfect!!

Hot summer nights were *our* ("our" meaning my brothers and me) time to explore the neighborhood and kind of live our own life. It's funny. We were always walking everywhere—miles and miles sometimes without considering it—through the streets and fields and parking lots around our house (at the time we lived in Warr Acres). Back then, there would always be lots of FROGS everywhere. I guess they (the frogs) would also come out at night because it was too hot in the daytime. We could see them only while they were trying to cross the street, where they would often get run over by cars and be a completely splattered little pile of unrecognizable guts.

We (my brothers and I) loved playing with frogs. They have such a great texture, and they're so cool-looking, and they are *soooo* mellow, and, yeah, we LOVED 'em (still do). It would make us sad to see so many of them run down on a nightly basis. Oftentimes, we could look ahead and see wet blood reflecting in the car headlights and would come across a frog that was still alive but dying ... it would be horrible and devastating.

So we began to do what we called "Frog Patrol," a nightly frog "search and rescue" kind of mission. We would go out and look for as many frogs as we could find that needed help getting out of the street. We would take a flashlight (but, funny, we didn't take paper towels or anything to grab 'em with), and just swoop up every frog we saw in the street and put it in the yard, sometimes in a panic—running *ahead* of cars as they drove down the street and trying to get the frogs out of the path of the tires.

I still do it now, if I see a frog (there are not very many these days) or, really, any creature that needs a helping hand. For instance, there is a very particular time of early summer that TURTLES like to scurry across the Turner Turnpike (the route I take up to Tulsa), but it's not at night—it's mid-morning. It's a particularly bad struggle for them (the turtles) because they are so SLOW and the cars are going so FAST (seventy-five miles per hour is the posted speed limit). And because it's a high-traffic highway, it is, for the "Turtle Patrol" rescuers, sometimes a hazardous dash to get out into the middle of the highway and grab 'em. There was one time, on my drive to Tulsa, that I was in quite a hurry, but I saw a big turtle creeping along the shoulder. I thought, *Maybe I should stop and put him back up in the grass.* But like I said, I was in a hurry. I kept driving. After a few more minutes, it began to worry and haunt me, and later, when I was on the trip back to OKC (that's Oklahoma City, where I live), I saw another big turtle on the shoulder of the highway, and in my mind I said, *Maybe that is the SAME turtle I saw a couple hours ago.* I pulled the car over and went to grab him, but he scuttled suddenly right out onto the highway. I stood and watched as the first car barely missed him, but the second one completely and instantly splattered him. Some of his blood drops even made it as far as landing on my shoe. *Maybe the other one lived.*

KATHY LOCKER

Kim Doner holds a raccoon rescue, one of many critters she has helped through WING-IT, a native wildlife rehabilitation organization in Tulsa, Oklahoma.

Rocky Ride

KIM DONER

N O O N E E V E R warned me that becoming Snow White
would lead to a life-or-death situation involving raccoons and Rice
Krispies Treats.

No, not the Snow White who is awakened by the Prince and lives
happily ever after, but the Snow White who dances, commiserates,
and plays with wildlife, *then* lives happily ever after (wildlife included).
Becoming a wildlife rehabilitator has brought me closer to this
childhood fantasy, yet when I share the achievement (and I even got a
"woodsman," lucky me!), the usual response is someone's countering
version of "when Grandpa had a pet raccoon."

To be honest, these tales make me cringe. Infant raccoons are great
fun, but they turn into *adult* raccoons—a whole different ball game.
And if you rehabilitate them properly from orphaned babies, they'll
be independent upon release, having grown from playful, snuggly,
engaging kits into relentlessly curious, voracious, feral little snots that
can morph into snarling masses of tooth and claw when thwarted.

In short, they are *raccoons*.

As a new rehabber, I'd spent time building experience with wildlife
as well as close friendships with those who shared my obsession. We
helped each other whenever possible. Case in point: Carol had three
young-adult orphans who were deemed independent and ready for
release, but she was stuck at home with two infant litters demanding
round-the-clock feedings. Shirley loved raccoons, had a perfect release

site (a cabin nestled on hundreds of acres of undeveloped woodland supplied with a burbling stream), and an offer. She and I could meet at her cabin that Friday, drink wine, release raccoons into the trees, drink more wine, grill chicken, and wave farewell to the masked marvels before bunking in. My inner Snow White reveled in anticipation.

I picked up three healthy—or perhaps a better term would be "hefty"—raccoons at Carol's, where they'd been coerced into pet carriers. I studied the crates as the contents bumped and scooted inside, bringing to mind the Looney Tunes character Taz when imprisoned. Chipped, dented, with logos scrubbed down to nothing and the threads stripped from the holding screws, the carriers had definitely seen their day. Carol had zip-tied the clamshell lids to the bases, then laughed about using another age-old trick to coax raccoons into such holding spaces: Rice Krispies Treats. And now an open box of the tasty bars sat beside me in the front seat.

Getting the raccoons back out of the carriers would be a sure shot later: just litter the path to freedom with Kellogg's finest, open the gates, and they'd be gone. No problem. The hard part was over; they'd been raised and readied, and all I had to do was arrive at the final destination.

The critters were behind me in my RAV4, a sheet draped over the kennels to reduce stimulus. Dark clouds loomed back in the west, but I was pretty sure I'd outrun any coming rain. All would be well, even though those little fellas trilled and growled and clawed the walls of their mini-prisons and I could hear miniature black hands rattle the gate latches. Then, as I hit rush hour traffic on the turnpike, thunder vibrated through the car, followed by a lightning crash and an Oklahoma downpour, the kind that initially slicks the streets and drums out other sounds with its fierceness. Well, *most* other sounds.

Slashing rain or not, I was determined. It would be an hour's journey, maybe more, considering the wet haze blanketing the lane ahead of me. Still, I felt confident my carload of 'coons would arrive just fine. I almost picked up the cell phone to call Carol, just to let her know I was in control and all was just peachy. I glanced to the right to snag my purse but considered the torrent pouring across my windshield and had second thoughts. However, my brief view reminded me of the "farewell kit" Carol had packed for her charges: something irresistibly tasty for their future adventure and all. Something to which I am addicted.

Rice Krispies Treats.

I love Rice Krispies Treats. Carol was totally wasting them on raccoons, who eat everything—nasty, rotting stuff, like maggoty trash and dead birds and grubs. I couldn't believe she had sent a whole box just for them. I looked again, longing.

The rain poured and the traffic worsened. A gap allowed me to avoid the sideways waterfall from a neighboring semi, so I took it—but changing lanes forced me to maintain an uncomfortable speediness.

The crying stopped behind me. No more scratching sounds, either. Good deal. I figured they'd settle down and go to sleep. I could relax a bit. I knew they'd tire from fighting those carriers sooner or later. Ha! I was right.

I leaned back a little, took a deep breath.

My car seat began to mimic a pricey chair in the theater, the footrest steadily moving my legs forward like comfy loungers do.

But my Toyota doesn't have a footrest.

Why do I feel like there's a pillow behind my calves?

The pillow shifted, lifted a little, settled.

I took a split second to look down, not wanting to take my eyes off the road for too long. My breath snagged in my throat. I did not want to believe it. I glanced again.

Holy crap.

I was going seventy miles per hour, in a cloudburst, through five o'clock traffic—and had a raccoon lodged between my knees. A *wild* raccoon, not a pet. A raccoon *ready for release,* to go forth into the world, to wreak havoc as raccoons are meant to do.

Horror flooded my body as I realized further: *Omigod, look where that nose is—inches from my, my, uhhh, oh, I feel light-headed, please be a nice raccoon, don't chomp there, oh, Lord, what if it bites me in the crotch?*

I could see my obituary: "Woman wrecks car while having lap chewed by raccoon." Or *worse.* Now that I knew the manner of my death, my brain went haywire with future visions, wondering what sort of interpretations would be made of my mangled corpse intimately entwined with that of a raccoon.

The animal wriggled forward. Sharp little nails pierced my jeans as it hauled its body further up my thighs and eased into my lap, adjusting its rather rank fanny between me and the steering wheel. It patted the buttons on my shirt, rubbing them between sensitive paws to see if they were edible.

I weighed imminent damage. Ahead of and behind me, the car was pinned between a dump truck and a red pickup. To the side: hemmed in by two minivans, stuffed with children. Lives were at stake.

And beside me, within reach ... *hope!* I slowly retrieved a treat from the open box. Using my teeth, I tore it open, removed the bar, and murmured, "Hi, there, little one ... wanna be my friend?" as I waved it under a pointed nose.

The lure was ignored. My heart sank. I was doomed. I had

seconds, minutes at best, left to my life. If a raccoon isn't interested in junk food, the rehabber has no powers left.

So I did the only thing left to do, the action any other all-American, red-blooded woman would take. With no alcohol available, I opted for the next-best choice. I crammed the entire Rice Krispies bar in my mouth. If I was going to die, I was going to consume a last crumb of life's joys.

I chewed.

He/she/it began to explore the new territory. The animal slid paws upward to hoist itself higher, gazing into my face as we hurtled through the downpour.

A cold, damp snoot bumped my chin, sniffed my breath. Claws latched onto my shirt. Acting "normal" was beyond me; what's "normal" in that situation? I worried about my nose and ears. I'd seen these predators rip into meat.

Faces are meat. Don't look at him. Her. It. Just breathe. And chew. This is not good.

I could feel my pulse pounding in my ears, and my breath came in little short pumps. My bloodless death grip on the wheel brought a whole new meaning to the phrase "white knuckling."

But then a sign from the universe: *Exit!* And soon! Which meant muscling into non-existent spaces and bullying my way to the far lane.

I would do this.

Using my last nerve, I lurched my way into the next lane. Unhappy honks.

Two lanes to go.

I chewed. I focused. The raccoon studied my face.

My move had intimidated a minivan. Its hesitation gave me another shot; I twisted the car in front of it. More honks.

The raccoon extended a finger. It slid the finger up my nose. You know—*just checking.* One never knows what's up there, does one? That is, if one is a raccoon.

Stay focused, stay focused, you're driving, just do that and chew. Enjoy your last meal, dammit! Think about something else. Like your new obituary: "Woman dies with booger-picking raccoon."

I managed another lane; one to go, the exit rapidly approaching. To my relief, the animal withdrew its paw from where it toyed with my right nostril, but not to climb down. No such luck. It used the free hand to grab my shoulder and pull its round fuzzy body up to sit there. He / she / it rifled through my scalp, such efforts causing hairs to shed from its thick fur and stick to my now sweaty neck.

A giddy part of my mind wondered if it actually *had* found fleas. *Dying with fleas in my hair is not nearly as bad as dying with raccoon teeth in my crotch, right? See, Kim, you can always find a bright side!*

One more lane.

Years ago, I'd discovered my inner sailor when I'd broken my ankle and lay there like a flipped turtle, swearing. Now I got to discover my inner Indy 500 driver as I jerked my steering wheel to the right and flew onto the exit ramp.

Easing to a stop, I turned off the ignition and exhaled, seeing my breath fluff the stripes of the full, fuzzy tail waving before my face. We sat that way for a few *loooooong* minutes, me and my new BFF.

I was alive. We were alive.

More deep breaths proved unnecessary as I geared up to capture, re-cage, rig a dilapidated crate, and return to the rainy traffic; it all fell into place (to my astonished gratitude). An hour later, the clouds broke as I turned onto the gravel drive; Shirley stood on the cabin's porch, waving my full glass of wine. Blinding sunshine flooded the car.

I shut off the engine, opened my door, tumbled out, and kissed the ground. Releasing that little s**t would feel fabulous. It did feel fabulous.

We opened the crates soon thereafter, toasting three fat bottoms with striped tails as they scrambled up the nearest tree to play and climb all night. Raccoons being *raccoons*. I put my feet up and took a drink, recognizing all the mixed feelings I experience when wildlife is released: hope for them, appreciation for sharing a moment of their lives, joy, relief, and often a little grief that they've moved on.

Oh, and smugness.

A big, fat helping of smugness.

Which goes beautifully with wine and a box of Rice Krispies Treats.

Delia Ephron considered Honey to be of the
"FWD," or "fluffy white dog," variety.

Photograph by © ELENA SEIBERT, 2018

Dogs

DELIA EPHRON

MY DOG'S NAME is Honey Pansy Cornflower Bernice Mambo Kass.

She has more than one name because, when I was about twenty, I was having a hamburger, fries, and a Coke in a coffee shop near my apartment. I was hanging out with friends, but I was drinking my soda the way I did with my parents—sipping it slowly to make it last the meal. Suddenly it hit me: *I'm on my own. I can have more than one Coke. If I can afford it, I can have two Cokes, and, if I don't care if my teeth rot, three.* This was a pivotal growth moment that somehow led fifteen years later to giving my first dog thirteen names. And my second dog, six. (The second-born's arrival never gets as much attention as the first; that's my sense of it as a second-born myself. The second-born is sweeter, however, at least in the case of my dog.)

At this point it is only fair to say that if you don't have a dog, you might want to skip to the next essay. Talking about one's dog can be as boring as people talking about their grandchildren. Dogs are the dog owners' revenge on grandparents—unless you have a dog and grandchildren, too, in which case you are a double threat in the boredom department. There are apparently some seventy-seven million dog owners in this country, which adds up to a lot of boring talk, a portion of which I am responsible for (much as it pains me to admit it because, in the family I grew up in, being called boring was like being called an ax murderer). I might have that statistic wrong. Perhaps it's seventy-seven million dogs, not dog owners. I can't keep facts straight. Numbers especially. Either way, it's an awesome statistic.

I did not grow up with dogs. For a short time we had two ducks. I or one of my sisters won them at a carnival. They were very cute yellow ducklings and they grew up in a flash to be very large white ducks. (I know it's obscene to have city children win baby farm animals, but that's what happened at the spring carnival at El Rodeo elementary, and, as far as the fifties go, that was the least of it.) They lived in the garage and swam in a small inflatable kiddie pool until they disappeared one night. I have no idea what happened to them. Most likely my parents had a hand in it, or possibly a roving dog, which is what we were told. We didn't mourn them. Also I had two very small turtles, Sunshine and Moonglow (possibly also won at a carnival), and it pains me to confess I let the water dry up in their bowl. In other words, I killed them.

Twelve or so years later, when I was taking a required science class in college, I had to cut a planaria in half. A planaria is a flatworm and, if you cut it in half, it regenerates, grows another head and tail. I cut mine in half, went off to Yale for the weekend, and when I returned my planaria was dead. There was a note from my professor. *I didn't think you were the sort of person to let a planaria die.* But he was wrong. Because of Sunshine and Moonglow, I knew that I was exactly the sort of person to let a planaria die.

I got a dog because my friend Deena got a dog. That's one of the best things about friends. Because they do something, you do something— something wonderful that you would never do. At the time I was married and living in Los Angeles with my two stepchildren. (And just as an aside, if you are a stepparent, rush right out and get yourself a dog. Because it's very nice to have someone in the house that loves you.)

We had Daisy, a rescue, for thirteen years. She was part Tibetan Terrier, which probably means nothing to you, but she had a coat of white and brown fur so soft and beautiful, you could wear it to a ball. She was about twenty-five pounds (not too big, not too small). Truly gorgeous.

Like gorgeous people, she knew she didn't have to work hard to get attention. People on the street fell all over her, drivers shouted out of car windows, "What is she?" "A mutt," I would shout back, knowing I had the most beautiful mutt in the world. Whenever I walked her, she would bark at the wind. This never failed to enchant me. In truth, however, she was a bit of a withholding dog, not one for a cuddle or a kiss.

We lived in Los Angeles longer than we should have because I couldn't bear to put Daisy in the cargo hold of an airplane. Then the Northridge quake happened.

I had never been in a big earthquake. Only a small one where the ground trembled in a soft roll and you might even ask someone, "Was that an earthquake?" and then call a friend and say, "I was just in an earthquake," as if something titillating had happened. When this quake, 6.7 on the Richter scale, struck at 4:31 a.m., we were jolted awake by violent shaking. We lived twenty miles away from the epicenter. Still, it was fearsome.

While we were sitting around in the dark afterward (all the lights had blown) waiting for aftershocks and listening to the relentless blare of car alarms set off by the tremors, I said to my husband, "If I die tomorrow, I want to die in New York." No more "Daisy doesn't get on a plane." She had a tranquilizer and survived. Back she moved with us to New York City and she preferred it as we did if you don't count the time a huge, hideous dog living in the apartment next door tried to murder her in the elevator.

Then she got old and sick and died.

That's what dogs do. They die on you.

Which is why I avoid reading most dog memoirs, because the dog always dies. And I weep buckets, which I did when Daisy died. I wept and wept and wept and wept.

After that I moped over dog adoption websites. Then I compulsively watched *Crossing Over*. This show had a popular run on cable in 2000 or so, around the time I was grieving for Daisy. Psychic John Edward (not to be confused with political John Edwards) stood in front of a live studio audience and connected with their "loved ones" who had "passed."

John Edward really did know remarkable things about people who had passed. About hydrangeas they loved or a miniature Christmas tree in a box, or that a woman met her husband on a tennis court, or that a death was violent, a knife involved. He made peace for everyone, and everyone wanted to see their relatives in the afterlife, which I wouldn't think is true for all people (but was true for anyone who wanted show tickets). Then I started watching *The Pet Psychic* with Sonya Fitzpatrick, an eccentric Englishwoman. Sonya communicated with dogs, cats, birds, primates, pretty much any animal. Lots of them had miserable pasts, tied up, starved, it was heartbreaking. All the dogs were big on wanting their owners to know they were grateful for finally having a happy life. The pets were always saying thank you, thank you, thank you. (Unlike children.) Once, as I recall, sensing a llama wanted to wear her silk scarf, Sonya tied it around the animal's long neck. After they were done communicating, the llama's owner tried to untie the scarf. "She wants to keep it," said Sonya, just as the llama whacked him with her head and knocked him over.

Then there was a psychic summit, which I also watched. John Edward from the Sci-Fi Channel network along with his wife and his two fluffy white dogs went to visit Sonya on Animal Planet. Edward and his wife wanted to get Sonya to find out why their dogs were peeing and pooping (she called it "whoopsing") indoors. She didn't get anywhere with that, but she did know that one of the dogs, Jerily (I think that's his name) always liked his biscuits broken up into little pieces. Both dogs were wondering about the floor. It turned out the Edwards were installing new flooring. The dogs wanted to know if there would be any carpet, which they preferred. Also a weird shoe thing came up. One dog asked about "the one shoe." The Edwards had recently opened a baby present and instead of two shoes, a pair, there had been only one. The dog "told" Sonya he wanted the shoe.

What I really want to say about my watching all this is that having a dog/loving a dog/losing a dog turned me into a nut.

What a remarkable love it is if I wept buckets and still wanted another, knowing the new one would die on me, too. That's possible anyway with anyone—that they might die first—but with dogs, it's nearly inevitable. Dog years. They're teenagers, according to my vet, at one and a half or two. They are simply so glorious when they're around.

I saw a documentary on television about how adaptable dogs are. They've figured out humans and how to connect with them. Unlike wolves. You can't turn a wolf into a dog no matter how hard you try, which is a lesson about bad boyfriends.

Honey, a Havanese, was not a rescue, which I feel guilty about, but she is a perfect dog—affectionate, friendly, mostly obedient.

As we were driving up I-95 to Royal Flush Havanese in Charleston, Rhode Island, I read *Dog Training for Dummies*, about how to pick a puppy suitable for an old retired couple, which sounded right to me. And I share. First of all, get a girl. I'm not certain that was in the book, maybe it's simply my prejudice. Second of all, hold the puppy and turn it over on its back. It should resist for a second—its legs will wave around—and then relax (showing that it trusts you). Also the puppy should walk toward you with its tail down, a sign of respect. That means you will dominate the dog and the dog won't dominate you. Honey did all those things, and the other puppies did not. One walked away and the other jumped all over us.

Among other things, having a dog provides a more entertaining form of junk e-mail. Along with being inundated with pleas and requests from Guy Cecil, Joe Biden, Chuck Schumer, Planned Parenthood, and the American Red Cross, today I got an e-mail inviting Honey to participate in a dog shedding competition. It wasn't about hair. Honey doesn't shed, anyway. It was a dog reality show like *Biggest Loser.* Shedding meant pounds. Many dogs are overweight, no surprise. Who can resist giving a dog a treat? They fixate. They stare you into submission. Honey, who weighs seventeen pounds, weighs two pounds too much. That is quite a lot. Without telling you my weight, let me put it this way: Honey losing one dog pound is like my losing fourteen. I didn't enroll her, however. Much as I love my dog, she is not a career.

Recently, to see how insane the dog world can be, I went over to the preliminary judging of the super fancy Westminster Dog Show. It took place in the huge warehouses used for exhibition on the Hudson River piers. In addition to rings where you could see the dogs parade around while being judged, a huge portion of the space was given over to dogs being prepared to show. As far as the eye could see were rows of dogs on tiny tables getting blow-dries. The dogs were being brushed, combed, and flat-ironed. Lots of flat-ironing. They were being sauced with whipped cream mousse and styling cream, sprayed with Tresemmé Extra Firm. The fur around their mouths—their doggie beards—was parceled into tiny ponytails, wrapped in cloth and secured with rubber bands, to be certain no eye gunk migrated there, dirtying their faces, turning them into, well, dogs. When the trainers showed the dogs, trotting them around the ring, most had hairbrushes tucked into the back waist of their pants or skirts, and the minute there was a break, the trainer whipped out the brush and gave the dog a sprucing. One other weird thing: While the dogs were awaiting their turns, the trainers frequently bit off a bit of treat in their mouths and gave it to them. In other words, the intimacy was a tad freaky. I hope those treats were actual chicken or cheese, and not yam and venison treats in the form of brown bricks, which is what Honey gets (the only other food she is allowed besides kangaroo).

When I returned home, the second I opened the front door, I heard the thumpety-thump of Honey's paws on the stairs—there is no sweeter sound—and then she appeared looking like a dirty shag rug in someone's garage. Show dogs have as much in common with dogs as dolled-up little girls in pageants do with little girls.

When Honey was about five, we had a pet psychic over, who charged quite a bit, at least as much as one month's telephone bill. The ostensible reason for this visit was that I had written a screenplay about a pet psychic and wanted to meet one.

Just as an aside I want to tell you about this screenplay, *Sammy*, because it's one of my favorites and it never got made. The setup: a woman who talks to animals falls in love with a man who talks to the dead. Only thing is, she can actually do it and he can't. Because he's a fraud, he thinks she's a fraud. Because she's for real, she thinks he's for real. The man has a dog, Sammy. The dog falls in love with the woman and rats him out. As I mentioned, it never got made, but at least, because I have included it here, it exists, albeit briefly.

My friend Carol recommended Jocelyn the pet psychic. Jocelyn had met Carol's dog, Dainty, and told Carol why Dainty didn't want to pee on a certain patch of grass but would be happier peeing on another patch. This turned out to be absolutely true and solved a BIG PROBLEM. Jocelyn, a lovely woman in her, I'm guessing, late thirties, was not peculiar in any way except, of course, she could communicate with dogs.

Honey liked her immediately, but Honey likes everyone except really tall people. Whenever anyone new comes over, Honey dances on her hind legs. Isn't that remarkable? Jocelyn immediately pronounced Honey a happy dog with no traumatic past, which we knew. She sat on the rug and observed Honey. After I mentioned Honey's incredible attachment to one of her squeaky toys, a gorilla, Jocelyn said that Honey didn't mind that she wasn't a mother, but she did want a litter of squeaky toy gorillas. Then Jocelyn said to me, "Honey is worried about your left thigh."

The week before, I had had a little growth taken off my left thigh, which turned out to be benign. There was a Band-Aid on the tiny wound, all hidden under my jeans. There was no way Jocelyn could have known about it.

This was startling. And not just because there was no way Jocelyn could have known about it. As irresistible as Honey is and as vulnerable (she trembles in a rainstorm), I have never thought of her as a dog that would run for help if I slipped in a shower or fell through, say, thin ice on a skating pond. I would guess she'd be thinking, *Is it time for lunch, and why aren't you giving it to me?* But apparently not. Apparently I have a really sensitive dog.

Because of the left thigh business, we took Jocelyn seriously and got Honey five more squeaky toy gorillas. They were hard to find online because it turned out they weren't gorillas, they were chimps. (We know the difference between a gorilla and a chimp, but when it comes to squeaky toys, it's hard to tell.) They continue to be the only squeaky toys she likes. She seems to know they are all alike and different from her other toys. Isn't that remarkable?

Honey's tricks: She can burrow under the covers and lie there like a lump.

That's about it.

Except one Sunday last winter, an amazing thing happened. Actually it started the Sunday before. I was making buttermilk pancakes, which I always do on Sunday mornings, and when I put butter on the griddle and turned on the burner, the griddle got so smoky it set off the smoke alarm. Honey went crazy—the piercing sound was painful to her sensitive doggie hearing. She tried to climb my legs. I picked her up and carried her out, and she clung, her little paws digging into my shoulder. The next Sunday, seven whole days later—are you following this?—I took out the griddle, put on some butter, turned on the burner, and Honey tried to climb my legs.

She must have associated the burner with the shriek of the alarm. Or the butter with the shriek, or the pancake griddle with it. The first week the alarm went off at least three minutes after the burner was lit and the butter melted. The second time, the alarm never went off. Still she made the connection.

Isn't she brilliant?

Now you can tell me all about your grandchildren. Or your cat.

*Reyna Grande stands in front of outstretched
monarch wings at a butterfly pavilion in Mexico City.*

A Migrant's Story

REYNA GRANDE

EVERY YEAR, MILLIONS of monarch butterflies migrate
from Canada to Mexico, where they spend their winters. They face
many perils along their nearly 3,000-mile journey: unpredictable
weather, pesticides, low supply of milkweed, loss of habitat. Despite
the traumatic experiences before, during, and after the journey, the
monarch knows that its migration is the only way to ensure the
survival of the next generation, and the next.

As a former undocumented immigrant, I have long admired the
monarch butterfly's will to live. For the monarch and for me and for
the millions of people in the world forced to leave their homelands,
migration is an act of survival. The monarch butterfly has become
a powerful symbol for the undocumented-immigrant community. It
serves as a reminder that every living thing on Earth deserves to thrive
in peace and harmony, that for both insect and human, migration is not
a crime but a necessity.

In my garden in Los Angeles, I planted milkweed and other flowering
plants to provide a safe haven for the local monarch population and
do my part to protect this magnificent creature. I shared my love of
gardening with my daughter, Eva, who was seven years old at the time
of this story, and while we weeded or planted bulbs, I would talk to her
about the plight of the monarch population. I told her that twenty years
ago, over a billion monarchs would make the journey south. Now their
numbers are at the lowest they've ever been. As with all migrants, their

struggle to survive is harder today than ever before. We humans are plowing away more and more land and leaving no room for milkweed or nectar plants, spraying harmful pesticides on our farmlands, and cutting down the forests where the monarchs spend their winters. "Something needs to be done," I told my daughter. Eva said that she would grow up to be an entomologist. "I'll save the monarchs," she declared.

She squealed in delight every time a butterfly visited our garden. I explained to her that they were laying eggs in the milkweed we had planted for them. When we watched a documentary about butterflies, Eva could no longer wait until she grew up to save them. She had to start that very day with our local population. She wanted to carry out a rescue mission to save the monarchs from the only threat she could see in our pesticide-free garden—predators.

Eva and I began to gather the milkweed leaves that had tiny eggs attached to their underside and put them in containers, safe from the spiders and praying mantises that lived in the garden. Once the caterpillars were grown, we transferred them to a butterfly habitat where they pupated before our eyes. Those three minutes of watching a yellow-black-and-white-striped caterpillar transform into a brilliant emerald-green chrysalis were magical. We gasped at seeing the tiny gold spots and a golden ring shimmering around the chrysalis.

Eva kept a journal where she wrote down every detail, and she learned to predict when the butterflies would be born. During the next ten days, we watched in awe as the chrysalis became transparent until we could see the black-and-orange butterfly nestled within. We released the new butterflies in the garden the same day they were born. To Eva, every butterfly was a girl, and she always gave them names. We would wave goodbye and wish them a safe journey. "Bye, Pearl. Bye, Sunshine. Come visit soon."

Standing beside my daughter, I felt connected to her through this shared experience. We'd been part of the cycle of life of this precious insect and bore witness to its metamorphosis.

One September day, one of the caterpillars did not attach itself securely enough to the roof of the butterfly habitat. In the middle of pupation, the chrysalis fell to the floor, and when we found it, one side was flat. My daughter and I used tape to hang the cocoon as carefully as we could, but when the monarch emerged from its chrysalis, its right wing was shorter than its left.

"I'm afraid we can't release it," I told my daughter. "She won't be able to fly."

A healthy monarch had a difficult road ahead in her fight for life. A monarch who couldn't fly was doomed.

"I will teach Buttercup to fly," Eva said.

I didn't have the heart to tell my daughter that it was not possible. How could a human teach a butterfly to fly, especially one with a severe disability?

Every day, Eva would take Buttercup out to the garden and place her on the butterfly bush to drink nectar and enjoy the sunlight. She would sit Buttercup on her index finger and raise her hand up and down to get wind under Buttercup's wings. Buttercup would take off into the air only to fall seconds later. Eva would pick her up from the grass and try again.

For several days, Eva put out fresh orange slices for Buttercup, and when the sun had warmed the garden, she would take her out to eat nectar and practice flying. I watched from the window, wondering how to prepare my daughter for the inevitable. Buttercup would spend the rest of her too-short life with us. She was never going to fly.

This butterfly, like me, had been born to struggle, something that my children knew nothing about. I had been born with a great disadvantage, too—an undocumented child immigrant from Iguala Mexico, in the state of Guerrero, where 70 percent of the population lived in poverty. No one thought I could escape the circumstances I had been born into. But I had. Just like the monarch leaves her home to give her offspring a chance, I had left the country of my birth, risked my life to cross the border, and made the impossible possible—I went from being an undocumented immigrant to a successful published author.

Because of my own migration to seek a better life in the US, I spared my children the trauma of being born in a shack made of sticks and cardboard, living without running water, walking around barefoot for lack of shoes, being hungry in every way. I spared my children the trauma of running across the border, the paralyzing fear of being caught and sent back or, worse, of perishing in the act of crossing. My children will never know what it's like to be labeled a "criminal" for simply wanting a better future, a chance to dream. They will never know the stigma of growing up undocumented, the trauma of trying to hold on to your roots while trying to assimilate into a new culture. They won't know the searing pain of a heart as it cleaves in two, fighting to maintain its Mexican identity while transforming into an American.

Like my story, the monarch's is one of struggle and survival.

As I watched my daughter share the fight with Buttercup and learn of perseverance and faith, I hoped that her love for this butterfly would be the magic formula that would help Buttercup fly.

A few days later, from the living room window, I watched my daughter do her usual routine. When she placed Buttercup on her finger and raised her hand up, Buttercup took off and soared into the air. I was expecting her to fall back down, but this time she didn't. She flew across the garden and over the neighbor's fence.

I rushed outside and watched as Buttercup disappeared from sight. Eva's face was full of triumph and pride.

"She did it!" Eva said. "She flew!"

"She did," I said. "She really did."

I don't know where Buttercup ended up. My daughter believes that her butterfly defied fate and went on to have a fulfilling life. I was happy to know that at least for this one moment, my daughter might have had a glimpse into my life. She witnessed firsthand what it's like to rise above the circumstances one is born into and find the strength to survive.

© KAREN KUEHN

Joy Harjo and a horse friend enjoy the sunset as she clutches a Native American flute. Both horses and flutes are recurring images in Harjo's music and writing.

Redbird Love

JOY HARJO

We watched her grow up.
She was the urgent chirper,
Fledgling flier.
And when spring rolled
Out its green
She'd grown
Into the most noticeable
Bird-girl.
Long-legged and just
The right amount of blush
Tipping her wings, crest
And tail, and
She knew it
In the bird parade.
We watched her strut.
She owned her stuff.
The males perked their armor, greased their wings,
And flew sky loop missions
To show off
For her.
In the end
There was only one.
Isn't that how it is for all of us?

There's that one you circle back to—for home.

This morning

The young couple scavenge seeds

On the patio.

She is thickening with eggs.

Their minds are busy with sticks the perfect size, tufts of fluff

Like dandelion, and other pieces of soft.

He steps aside for her, so she can eat.

Then we watch him fill his beak

Walk tenderly to her and kiss her with seed.

The sacred world lifts up its head

To notice—

We are double, triple blessed.

In Honor of Mo Who Is Our Cat, and We Are Hers

First we heard her heart,
a motor larger than her small mew self;
it filled her up, then us
when we touched.
And then the room
everything in the room:
couch, windows, the door
and eventually every room in the house
and the yard
and beyond the yard to the many years
of our lives—
This Mo
revealed herself a hunter:
of mouse
of roaches and any crawling thing
of birds
(most she could not catch and we
—the birds and us—were grateful)
of sunlight,
dog and plant leaf,
feet under blankets,
cords, wires
and laps and even computers—

This Mo became the first to answer every door

and greet every visitor from beyond

especially those who dislike cats—

(those she greets most heartily

she has a sense of humor).

This Mo of catdom

in the winter grows

a stunning Siamese stole

she cleans daily to a shine

and gleam

and in the summer sheds it all

and stalks the house and yard

dressed ratty

in a jacket she still cleans

with fruitless effort—

This catward, forward Mo has weathered

the come and go of houses, dogs

and humans, the dragging her

and chasing her, and the

stealing of birds from the dominion of her

crying into her fur with her—

We know her as Mo: short for motor,

more better, more cat soul

per square or round inch—

most appreciative we are, and more.

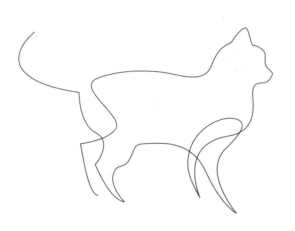

*Amy Hempel embraces her pit bull Gandhi, who
was adopted from the Connecticut dog rescue
Morgan's Place. What first began as a foster home
for Gandhi quickly became his forever home.*

Moonbow

AMY HEMPEL

PEOPLE ARE GETTING away with murder, but I can't get away with having a glass of water in bed. I trade sides with my dog, who won't feel what I spilled anyway.

From this side of the bed, I see the moon through the window. It's a full moon with—something extra. I've heard about this, but not in upstate New York—in Africa, where the mist from Victoria Falls on the night of a full moon can cause a rainbow to form, a white one: a moonbow. People book vacations to see it.

I head downstairs and out to the small backyard. Who else is seeing this? And then I see who else: a small brown bear, or maybe it's black. I freeze, trying not to look scared because that's when they attack, I'm told. A bear is moving calmly from the neighbor's yard into mine. He looks up at the moon; we look at it together. The bear drops to the ground and then stands up pawing a ball. It belonged to my dog, the other one, who died the month before. The bear sees the dog's water bowl that I keep filled from habit or hope and helps himself to a drink. He wraps himself in the rope from the old tie-out. He swipes at the gone dog's favorite plush toy, a damp, matted lamb with the squeaker torn out.

The bear rolls on his back under the freakish white rainbow, kicking his feet like one other creature I knew. "Logan?" I ask, moving a step closer. "It's all right."

I tell him what has happened since I lost him, and assure him that I approved of his valedictory bite, that awful deliveryman who had it coming. I tell him that the deli has gone up for sale, that another antiques store has opened, that I hate my haircut, that I have not thrown anything away, that the water in the kitchen has developed a metallic aftertaste.

And then the bear is leaving. On his feet and moving to the back of the yard, he stops by the old rope swing. I think he's going to put his legs through the tire and push off toward the moon, but then I see he's got the rope between his teeth. He chews and shakes his head until he has chewed through the rope and the tire falls to the ground where the bear kicks it out of his way as he tears off through the woods.

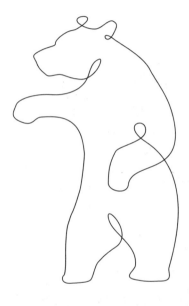

THALIA ARENAS

Juan Felipe Herrera adopted these two shepherd-mix
puppies, Canela and Chubby, from the Central California
SPCA to help them find their permanent homes.

Letter to Sudan: Last White Male Rhino on Earth

JUAN FELIPE HERRERA

For the veterinary team, wildlife rangers, and conservancy workers of Ol Pejeta
Conservancy in Nanyuki, Kenya, who took care of you.

You are gone now—
       the one who

ate thin reeds the color of rain & wondered
about your daughter
Nadine &
Fatu your granddaughter   what will happen to them
& the moist red-brown lands of Africa
you will roam there
          in another realm

     your full horn will turn
through the bluish-white
storms once again
  breeze

& the rhino tribes
brothers in shadow & sisters with cut-off faces
by the poacher men—gone all gone

bleeding w/o horn—   sold for promise money
sour magic man-juice & tourist luxuries

                                        you

come back Sudan—Northern White
in each one of us
        circle infinity now
                kindness as you lay
on the kindness of grasses

*S. E. Hinton has a passion for horseback riding,
which has influenced much of her work. Her
Dutch Warmblood, Ritzy, is just one of the
horses she has shared her life with over the years.*

Baby Horse

S. E. HINTON

MY FIRST LOVE was horses, so it's not surprising my first child was a horse. When I was twenty years old, I took the last seventy-five dollars in my bank account and bought a four-month-old colt. My logic was: Where else would I get a horse for seventy-five dollars? I knew nothing about training horses, and this colt had never even had a halter on. But how hard could it be? I was good with animals, had ridden off and on since I was five and was decent at it, and surely I could scrape up enough money for board every month.

The man I bought him from was a school superintendent; he had his high school football team herd the colt into a horse trailer. He advised me to use some milk supplement with his grain since he was really too young to be weaned, dropped him off in the stall I had rented, and drove away.

There I was with my baby, and I had never changed a diaper.

He stood at the back of his stall with his face to the wall. I stood near his feed box, poured his feed, and talked to him. He was a pretty bay with a single white T on his forehead—three-quarters Thoroughbred, one-quarter Quarter Horse. Hunger and curiosity brought him closer. I didn't attempt anything other than talk the first few days.

My favorite book in those days was *Gone with the Wind,* and I named him Rhett. But I called him Baby Horse.

Eventually I got in the stall with him. I put a halter on him, and he didn't mind. I practiced leaving him tied for longer and longer periods. I brushed him. He was much more patient when I was talking to him.

Soon I could lead him around. Since there is not much you can do with a colt that young, I taught him to lunge. By the time he was six months old he would walk, trot, canter, halt, stand, and walk on the lunge line. He also had a great vocabulary. And he was especially tuned in to praise.

Like any mother, I wondered what he'd like to be, what classes he could take—he could decide. Barrel racer? Trail horse?

Then one day he was racing around with the other horses boarded there and took a three-foot fence without pausing.

"Okay," I thought, "jumping it is."

I put down a board in the corral and led him across it. After a while, I jogged him across it. Then I lunged him in a small circle near it. Then I attempted to lunge him over it.

All hell broke loose. You would have thought I'd asked him to leap into a volcano of molten lava. He reared. He shied. He fought the line. He delivered an Oscar-worthy performance of complete terror. Fortunately, by then, I was well aware that he wasn't scared of much.

Sure enough, soon he was jumping the board. Jumping the small jumps I made from whatever was lying around. And he was vastly insulted with any jump too low for his ego.

He was a drama king. When I left the barn, he literally tried to get in the car with me, almost sobbing. And when I'd lead him around the barn and pasture, he'd react with complete boredom—or a sudden shy of pretend horror, as if to say, *There's a bear in that bush! You're risking my life, leading me near bears!*

It never occurred to me that I had a demented horse. I thought it was cute. I reacted the way a mom would to a toddler involved with a bedtime book. Of course he had an imaginative narration going on in his mind. I did, too. We all entertain ourselves with exciting scenarios of Walter Mitty alternate lives.

But like most young mothers enamored with their first child, I thought, "He's smart! He's cute! He's beautiful!" I was well on my way to spoiling him rotten.

Larry Larson

"Excuse me, you have a very nice horse there, but you're ruining him. Would you please put him in training with me?"

I can remember distinctly the first words Larry Larson ever said to me.

My husband and I moved to Palo Alto in the early 1970s while David attended graduate school at Stanford. Naturally I hired horse transportation and had my baby horse shipped out to join us.

At that time, Larry was a fixture at Stanford Stables. He trained horses and gave lessons. Later he became a very well-known and beloved show judge, but then he was twenty-one, twenty-two, a few years younger than I was, and just getting started. I had seen him often, and so I answered, "Yes! Yes! Yes!"

My baby horse had gone from a spirited toddler who still loved his mother's praise to a belligerent teenager who didn't give a damn what his mother thought.

I had started easing onto his back when he was two, had him saddled and bridled at three. All was fine.

Then between four and five he discovered the joys of bucking. And bolting. And I discovered I didn't know nearly as much about riding as I had thought.

Larry was a godsend.

The first time Larry rode him he sent me away.

"You. Mom. Go stand over there and look away."

So that's what I did, cringing while Larry gave him probably his first taste of discipline.

And after that my baby horse would knock me down to get to Larry. He loved the man. *This guy knows what he's doing.* We had advanced to communicating almost telepathically. You don't get to choose your family. He was an Aries and made me nervous. I am a Cancer and I bored him. But still, when he was injured, or tired, he'd stand with his head on my heart while I comforted him, rubbing his neck and telling him what a wonderful baby horse he was.

"He's very clever," Larry said, "and too good for you. He needs to be with a better rider."

"I'll get better," I said. And I did.

Larry rode him in his first show, where he got a third in the three-foot open jumping. And he also gave him his show name. "He's like a little Toyota going around the courses with all those big trucks." In honor of Larry, Toyota became his name from then on.

I got a fifth on the flat class* of thirty-five, and my baby horse and I became hooked on showing. Larry took me to a tack store and helped me get my correct gear. He showed me how to fill out an entry form. Gave me tips on riding in a large crowd in a flat class.

By one of those strange coincidences in my life that happen far too often to be *just* coincidence, while I was writing this section, my husband was going through memorabilia in an old file cabinet and came across a letter from Larry, more than forty-five years old. It confirmed my memory that we were very close friends. He adored my baby horse, and I hadn't given him too much credit for changing my riding life.

Well, Stanford Stables is gone now, demolished for housing. Larry is gone and mourned by thousands. But our time there remains in my memory as magical.

Show Time

The first thing I did when we moved back to Tulsa after three years in Palo Alto was look for another trainer. I needed someone to take my horse over higher jumps, since the three-foot jumps I was doing bored him. And I certainly needed more lessons myself.

When I find someone who's compatible with me, I tend to stick with them. All in all, including Larry, I've had three riding trainers.

My baby horse did so many things I would have found extremely annoying in any other horse. Waiting in the lineup to be pinned in an under saddle class,* he would turn his head and nibble on my boot toe in an effort to make me talk to him. And when I let him graze outside the arena while the judges were deciding, he just *knew* I was standing on the most delicious grass ever grown.

I had noticed in practice that he drooped when made to do the same jump over and over. But if I talked to him in an excited voice, "Look we're about to jump," he'd perk up, pick up the energy, and actually jump instead of doing a half-hearted hop. Of course, I praised him accordingly.

One day, at an out-of-town show, I was sitting in the stands brooding over what a bad show I was having. My new trainer came by and said, "Well, did you drink your beer?"

I had learned a beer could take the edge off my nerves before a class.

"No."

"Did you talk to your horse?"

"No."

"Well, do it!"

It was Oklahoma hot, so I had my beer. And maybe a couple of others. We completed our course, in a class of thirty, then waited outside the ring to jog in, blue ribbon first, then red second, and so on to sixth.

It was taking an unusually long time to pin the class, but finally we were called. The baby horse and I had won! Then one of the judges came out of the stands to say something to me. Wow! We must have been really good.

"Congratulations, that was a very good round," he began, "but you have to stop talking to your horse. I don't mind a soft 'ho' in the corners, but please don't go, 'Oh look, a little green wall! Let's jump the little green wall!'"

That year, 1980, with my trainer up, the baby horse, a.k.a. Toyota, won the Regular Working Hunter State Championship.

The next year he had two careers. Show horse and movie star.

Toyota was already a famous hunter in Oklahoma when Disney contacted me about making a film of my novel *Tex*. I mentioned I had a horse perfect for the horse part, and he would do it for a credit. The director, Tim Hunter, had decided to shoot it in Bixby and Tulsa and thought this was a great idea.

We moved Toyota to a private Quarter Horse ranch so I could give the star, Matt Dillon, riding lessons for a couple of weeks before the film started shooting.

Matt is a natural athlete, and he was a fearless seventeen-year-old. Toyota loved him. If Matt teetered too far to one side, Toyota would move under him to help him regain his balance. Once I told Matt the horse was not used to a Western bit, and to ride him with a loose rein, he never relied on the reins for balance. He loved the fact that voice commands were enough: *walk, trot, canter, whoa* were basics in Toyota's vocabulary.

I had Matt keep carrots in his pockets, and there is a nice scene in the movie where the horse nuzzles him for them.

Toyota, meanwhile, *knew* all the lights, cameras, and people were there for him, personally, and behaved like the star he was. The production manager told me he had never seen a better behaved horse on camera. I was half surprised my baby horse didn't figure out a way to sign autographs.

Because of the movie, he missed half the shows where he could get points for Regular Working Hunter, but he won 1981 Reserve Champion anyway.

Toyota went on to win many ribbons and trophies over the years. He loved going to shows and neighed excitedly at the sight of a show trailer.

We'd finally learned to wire his show stalls shut; otherwise, he'd open the door and ramble through the aisles to poke around the tack stall for treats—or even to pick up a broom and try to push it.

When he was seventeen, he went lame, and his longtime vet, DeRoy White, couldn't discover the cause. (DeRoy's memory: *Not only is Toyota the only horse who ever got away from me—he did it twice.*)

I found him a great retirement home, run by a friend who lived on several acres and treated her animals like children. I visited every now and then to talk to him and sometimes ride him around bareback.

I have a nice video of my husband and my little boy taking him carrots for his twenty-first birthday.

"Animals are markers in our lives," I said to my aunt. We were visiting in Fort Worth to pick up a puppy for our eight-year-old. "When this dog dies, it will be the end of Nick's boyhood. Like when Toyota dies, it will be the end of my young adulthood."

When we reached home late the next night, there was a message on our answering machine.

Toyota was very ill—with severe colic.

I dropped puppy, suitcase, and family to rush to my horse.

The vet had already oiled him and recommended I walk him for a while. We both agreed he was too old to go through surgery.

I walked Toyota all over the pasture. I recounted his life to him: "Remember when you were a baby and you … that time Larry took you to that show…when you saved my life on that course … when you and Matt …"

The walking did no good. DeRoy stood by with the shot.

"Susan, maybe you better stand over there."

"You try and get me away from this horse!" I cried.

When he went down, toppling sideways, I was there next to him, making sure the last thing he heard was my voice.

"Goodbye, Baby Horse! Goodbye!"

Well, that *was* the end of my young adulthood, but I kept riding. I've had several horses since, some excellent, some not a good match. There were some I loved very much. I rode for thirty-five years in the ring, then took up trail riding for a few years.

A couple of years ago, some fairly serious surgeries finally put an end to my riding for good. Of course since riding was a major part of my life, I still dream about it.

Most often the horse in my dream is my baby horse.

In my dreams, he talks to me.

---

* In equestrian competition, "on the flat" and "under saddle" classes are non-jumping classes judged on the smoothness of the transition from one gait to another. On the flat classes judge the rider's ability to control the horse. Under saddle classes are judged based on the movement and disposition of the horse during competition.

JOHN M. PICKARD

Brandon Hobson and his dog Rango spend time together in their backyard—Rango's favorite place for chasing squirrels.

Sunlight Travelers

BRANDON HOBSON

1

IT HAD RAINED earlier that day, and the clouds were still
bulbous and drifting to the east when I arrived at Pets and People
Humane Society. I was there to adopt a dog. I was, among other things,
sad, and it was necessary, if not crucial, that I find a dog because back
then I was also very lonely. The volunteer had raven-black hair and a
dreamy nature despite speaking in a toneless voice, despite recognizing,
probably, that I felt bitter toward the world.

"I live in a small apartment," I told her, "so I need a dog already
house-trained. I'm not picky about breed."

I followed her to a terrier mix with a Jack Russell face but bigger
body, white fur with brown spots. She opened the cage and he let her
put the leash on him. I noticed his eyes and thought, *You might be the
envy and admiration of the others*. The volunteer told me he was skittish
and afraid, adding that his age was uncertain. They try to guess age
from looking at teeth, but she said he could've been two years old or
even six or seven.

"Well, age doesn't matter," I said.

She handed me the leash, and we went outside for a walk along
the road. Thunder rumbled in the distance, so we didn't walk too far.
Overhead, the sky was clearing, the clouds separating. He was calm,
which I liked. He was alert and excited to take a walk, and it seemed
he wasn't too afraid of me. As I knelt down to him I noticed his eyes,

again, were filled with an intolerable beauty. I gently scratched his head, assured then I would take him home. I have often thought that dogs are silent messengers from God, and as I looked at him I wondered what his message was for me.

The sun came out from behind a cloud.

2

THE VOLUNTEERS AT the shelter called him Topper, but I wanted something literary. I thought Rimbaud. I thought Voltaire, Vasko Popa. I finally decided on Chaucer.

He adjusted to my couch and slept at the foot of my bed. When I came home from work every day I could see him sitting at the window, looking out at the world. We took long walks through the neighborhood. We went to the city park. I ran along the jogging trail, holding the leash, Chaucer running beside me. I began to miss him while I was at work.

At home he followed me from room to room. He was so anxious in those early days. After a few obedience classes, I taught him to shake hands, wave, and give high fives. He liked to take walks and run, dig through leaves or branches or anything he could find outside. He was pleasant to my friends. If I took a nap, I would wake up and find him beside me. He slept beside me every night.

This is the kind of unconditional love that saw me through those few years when I was not happy with my job, or where I was living, or myself.

Soon enough, though, I noticed I became more at peace with myself, more observant to the world around me. In my small apartment I could see rays of sunlight slanting in and warming him from where he sat beside the window. He liked this warmth, especially in winter, because my apartment was not well insulated. I saw colors in this sunlight, as if reflected from stained glass, colors that came at various times during the day, but most often at sunset, when the sun on the horizon was pink or red. The light streaming in moved as if through branches, and I remember thinking how beautiful and magical that light seemed.

I found I could sit for long periods of time with Chaucer without watching television or listening to music. I found I was becoming less distracted by outside noise. I was becoming more parental, more responsible, and more patient.

This is how we were for a while, and soon life was no longer sad for me. A year or so later I met my wife and fell in love with her. She fell in love with me, too, and also fell in love with Chaucer.

He lived through our early years of marriage. He lived through my oldest son's birth and early childhood. He was always there with us.

Then he had to leave, of course. We lose loved ones in life, as all things eventually come to an end. But I had him for eleven years, and those eleven years were some of the happiest of my life.

The day before he left, I was finishing up a night class for my PhD when my wife called. "Chaucer's having seizures," she said. "I'm not sure what's happening. I went into the backyard and tried to hold him."

"Call the vet," I said. "Call someone, anyone."

It was an hour's drive home from campus.

That night it rained the whole drive home, and I sat with him until late, trying to comfort him. Our last evening together.

One of the joys of Chaucer in my life was his unconditional love, which was healing. I sometimes wonder what he thought when he saw me for the first time.

Did he recognize my reckless abandonment, my longing for companionship?

Today, my wife and I have two children and a rescue border collie/corgi/Chihuahua mix named Rango, who is a delight in our lives.

Dogs are like angels, visiting us in dreams after they're gone. When Chaucer visits me in my dreams, we're walking outside somewhere, or we're playing on the floor, as we used to do. The dreams involve bright days, full of sun. We are sunlight travelers, the two of us, always walking someplace together.

Sometimes, too, when it's raining, I will look to the sky, because rainy days aren't so bad anymore, and I know his spirit is there, watching and waiting. His spirit is both gentle and strong.

Here's what I know now: When he runs, I hear the thunder. When he speaks, I see the sun.

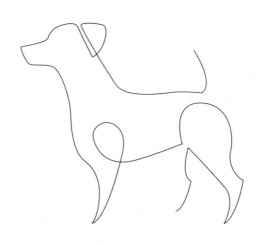

JERRY BAUER

Dean Koontz and his golden retriever, Trixie, have both written their fair share. Trixie "wrote" five books including, I Trixie, Who Is Dog, *to raise money for her fellow assistance dogs.*

A Spooky Moment Around Which the Entire Story Revolves

DEAN KOONTZ

THE SPOOKY MOMENT central to this story comes on an evening more than ten years ago.

Trixie, a three-year-old golden retriever of singular beauty and splendid form, adopted the previous September, is in her fourth month with my wife, Gerda, and me.

She is joyful, affectionate, comical, intelligent, remarkably well behaved. She is also more self-possessed and dignified than I had ever realized a dog could be.

Already and unexpectedly, she has changed me as a person and as a writer. I am only beginning to understand the nature of those changes and where they will lead me.

January 1999:

Our first house in Newport Beach, in the neighborhood known as Harbor Ridge, had an exceptionally long upstairs hallway, actually a gallery open to the foyer below. Because this hall was carpeted and thus provided good traction for paws and because nothing breakable stood along its walls, I often played there with Trixie on days when the weather turned foul and on cool winter evenings when the sun set early.

Initially, I tossed a ball and sometimes a Kong toy down the hall. The Kong was about six inches long, made of hard rubber with an inch-wide hole through the middle. You could stuff a mixture of peanut butter and kibble in the hole, to keep your dog occupied for an hour or longer. I tried this twice, but Trixie managed to extract the tasty mixture from the Kong in five minutes, which was less time than I took to prepare it.

One evening the rubber Kong bounced wildly and smashed into a small oil painting, splitting the canvas. The painting was very old, and it was one of Gerda's favorites.

When she noticed the damage a few days later, I fessed up at once: "The dog did it."

"Even standing on her hind feet," Gerda said, "the dog isn't tall enough to do it."

Confident that my logic was unassailable, I said, "The dog was here in the hall when the damage occurred. The Kong toy was here. The Kong belongs to the dog. The dog wanted to play. If the dog wasn't so cute, I wouldn't have wanted to play with her. Hall, dog, Kong, cute, play—the damage to the painting was inevitable."

"So you're saying the dog is responsible because she's cute."

I refused to allow my well-reasoned position to be nitpicked. I resorted to my backup explanation: "Besides, maybe she isn't tall enough, but she knows where we keep the step stool."

So, because the dog had damaged the painting, in subsequent play sessions in the hall, we could not use the rubber Kong. Furthermore, I would not throw the tennis ball anymore, but would only roll it.

I explained the new rules to Trixie, whose expression was somber. "This is a valuable teaching moment," I concluded. "You see, I'm sure, that if you had gone to your mother immediately after you damaged the painting and had taken responsibility, you would not now have this blemish on your reputation."

Following the new rules, I always released the tennis ball with a snap of the wrist that gave it the velocity to roll the length of the hall. Trixie thundered after the ball, either snaring it near the end of its journey or snatching it out of the air if it ricocheted off the leg of a console and took flight. She returned it to me with dispatch, and at once I fired it off again. After twenty minutes, her flanks heaved, her tongue lolled, and though she still considered the tennis ball to be a priceless treasure, she was prepared to entrust it to me for a while.

Lying on the floor, facing each other, Trixie panted and I stroked her luxurious golden coat as she caught her breath.

From the week she came into our lives, Trixie and I had spent some time most days lying on the floor together. I found it relaxing for the obvious reason that a cuddle with a loving dog is always calming. I also found it strange, because she would stare into my eyes as long as I wanted to meet hers—ten minutes, twenty, thirty—and she would rarely be the first to look away.

These sessions were meditation but also communication, though I can't explain what she communicated other than love. I can say that I frequently saw in her eyes a yearning to make herself understood in a complex way that only speech could facilitate.

Staring into Trixie's eyes, I was sometimes silent but at other times talked to her about my day, my problems, my hopes, whatever came into my head. Those who love dogs know well this kind of rap. The dog does not react—and is not expected to react—to any of this, but listens and wonders. Dogs swim through a sea of human speech, listening attentively for words they recognize, patiently striving to interpret what we say, although most of it is and

always will be incomprehensible to them. No human being would
have such patience. Counting the many commands she had been
taught when in training to be an assistance dog and all that she had
learned on her own—cookie, chicken, walk, duck, step stool, oil,
painting, restoration, electromagnetism—her vocabulary was at
least a hundred words. It would more than double over the years.
This got me thinking…. The recognition that words have meaning,
the desire to remember them, the intention to act on those that are
understood—does all of this lead to the conclusion that the dog also
yearns to speak?

On that January night, because Trixie had been an undiluted joy
during the previous four months and had already been a force for positive
change in me, I said, "You're not just a dog. You can't fool me. I know
what you *really* are."

As if in response, she raised her head, eased back slightly, and
regarded me with what might have been concern. Golden retrievers have
versatile brow muscles that allow them a wide range of facial expressions.
She never before responded to me in this fashion, and I was amused to
interpret her look as meaning, *Uh-oh, somehow I've blown my cover.*

"You're really an angel," I continued.

To my surprise, she scrambled to her feet as if in alarm, ran down
the hall, turned, and stared back at me. Muscles tensed, legs spread for
maximum balance, head lifted, ears raised as much as a golden can raise
them, she seemed to be waiting for what I might say next.

I'm seldom speechless. Trixie's behavior, which seemed to be a
reaction to my words, as if she understood every one of them, raised the
fine hairs on the nape of my neck and left me mute.

Intrigued, I got to my knees, wondering what she would do next, but
she continued to watch me intently when I rose to my feet.

For a minute or two we studied each other from a distance of twenty feet, as though we both expected something of consequence to happen. Her tail did not wag. It wasn't lowered as it would have been if she had been the least fearful. It was a perfect plume, as still as if she had stepped outside of time, where nothing could move her or even one hair upon her, nothing except her own will.

"Trixie?" I finally asked, and when I spoke, she retreated another ten or fifteen feet and turned again to face me in the same expectant stance as before.

This was not a dog who wanted solitude or even distance. The closer she could be to us, the happier she appeared. When I was writing, she would sometimes slink under my desk and curl herself into the shape of an ottoman, and she sighed with pleasure when I rested my stockinged feet on her. With Gerda even more than with me, this sixty-plus-pound creature behaved like a lapdog, most content when embraced.

This was the first and last time she wanted distance from me. As we stared at each other, I began to realize that regardless of what Trixie's behavior implied, if it implied anything at all, I should not pursue this matter further if only because it disturbed her. Besides, I was dealing here with the ineffable, the pursuit of which offers endless frustration but no reward other than the thrill of the chase.

I sat on the hallway floor, my back to the wall, legs straight in front of me, and I closed my eyes. The nape of my neck tingled for a while, but when the fine hairs stopped quivering, Trixie returned to me. She snuggled against my side. Putting her head in my lap, she allowed me to rub gently behind her ears and stroke her face.

Later, I told Gerda about the incident, but of course she could make no more of it than I could. We don't have paranormal experiences or go to psychics. We don't even read our daily horoscopes.

I write fiction for a living. I could spin a score of intriguing scenarios out of this one spooky moment with Trixie, but none would be as strange as the truth, if it could be known in this instance. Truth is *always* stranger than fiction. We craft fiction to match our sense of how things ought to be, but truth cannot be crafted. Truth *is,* and truth has a way of astonishing us to our knees, reminding us that the universe does not exist to fulfill our expectations.

Because we are imperfect beings who are self-blinded to the truth of the world's stunning complexity, we shave reality into paper-thin theories and ideologies that we can easily grasp, and we call them truths. But the truth of a sea, in all its immensity, cannot be embodied in one tide-washed pebble.

When we write a novel, concoct a new political system, devise a theory to explain the workings of the human mind or the evolution of the universe—we are fictioneers, bleaching the rich narrative of reality into a pale story that we can better comprehend. We go wrong when we don't admit the unknowable complexity of reality, but we go dangerously wrong when we claim that one pale story— or an anthology of them—is truth. We arrive at the paleness to *avoid* consideration of the daunting truth in all its fierce color and infinite detail.

I can never know the truth of that spooky moment with Trixie, but what I do know is that throughout the years she was ours to cherish, she continually surprised us, as truth will. She made us laugh every day, and at times we wept in anguish because of her. She weighed only sixty-something pounds, I occasionally called her Short Stuff, and she lived less than twelve years. In this big world, she was a little thing, but in all the ways that mattered, including the effect she had on those who loved her, she lived a big life.

In each little life, we can see great truth and beauty, and in each little life we glimpse the way of all things in the universe. If we allow ourselves to be enchanted by the beauty of the ordinary, we begin to see that all things are extraordinary. If we allow ourselves to be humbled by what we do not and cannot know, in our humility we are exalted. If we allow ourselves to recognize the mystery and the wonder of existence, our fogged minds clear. Thinking clearly, we follow wonder to awe, and in a state of awe, we are as close to true wisdom as we will ever be.

Trixie was innocent and joyful, but also at times enigmatic and solemn. I learned as much from this good dog as from all my years in school.

Jill McCorkle at age twelve, holding Smoky, circa 1971

Dogly Prayers and Wishes

JILL McCORKLE

IN A LONG LINE of dogs over the years, two have carried traces of divine intervention: Smoky, from my childhood, and Buster, of my children's childhood, and there's a way the two have blended in my mind to form a continuum, the root of which is desire, faith, and immortality.

Smoky was a stray, a black ball of fur resembling a bear cub (thus the name) who was found in a drainage ditch (we called it "the canal") where everyone in my neighborhood liked to play. I was about to go into sixth grade and not as frequent a participant in the canal games as I'd once been, but everyone knew that I had been begging for a dog and even sometimes "borrowed" a neighbor's beagle puppy and pretended he was mine for as long as they would let him stay. We had had a series of dogs by then, and the stories weren't happy ones. Tippy was a collie mix who was sent to a good home in the country, and, yes, I stupidly believed that for years, even after witnessing the dog catcher driving her to her new home. There was Eggmont, a basset who needed a temporary home and bayed interminably until that happened, and Babaloo, an inherited poodle who had been the most recent to break our hearts when she was hit by a car while trying to follow my sister and me along with several others from the neighborhood. We saw it happen, and we were squatted there with her as she died. The poor man who hit her was wringing his hands and offering a new dog, and saying, *Thank God, it wasn't one of you children,* and getting reassured by the adults who had gathered and agreed with him. It did not make me feel better, and it didn't resurrect Babaloo.

But what it did do—once the grieving was at bay—other than provide me with a story that got requested at sleepovers for several years to come when we all felt like sitting in a circle and crying, is set me off on an endless begging spree. At Christmas and at my birthday and many times in between, I asked for a dog, and each time, my parents told me that we would get a dog after we fenced in the yard and not until, that we couldn't go through a loss like Babaloo again. Then enter Smoky, who out of the blue was delivered to me by a younger member of the neighborhood who was seeking advice about what to do with him. This boy already had a beautiful collie named Sargent, who lived in *his* fenced backyard.

I told him to give me the puppy, and I would figure it out. I then brought him inside and announced to my mother that I would always believe in God because I had prayed for a dog and *look!* I knew what I was doing, of course; I was someone who had to be forced to go to Sunday school and any activities affiliated with church. It wasn't even a question of believing anything but a total dislike of tight itchy clothing and having to sit still and not laugh for an hour. *I prayed for him*, I told her. *He was sent to us.* I am pretty sure she knew that I knew what I was doing, too, but within minutes, she had taken him into the kitchen and run a sinkful of warm water. She told me to go get the Prell shampoo, and in no time, there he was, a new member of the family, the dog who would see my sister and me off to college and into our adult lives.

Smoky was maybe part Belgian shepherd, part chow. He had a blue tongue and a thick black coat, a curled tail, and dainty little legs. He once dug a cave under the roots of a tree so deep that when I sat in it, only my head was above ground and my toes couldn't reach the end. He knew that word *dig* and would do so on command (best said at the beach or some place where digging was not a big deal). He also knew *ball* and *snuggy*—a strange furry orange creature we had gotten for buying gas at the Gulf station—and the difference between the two. He understood *supper* and *snack* and *out*, and he knew *get him*, originally *get it*, but he easily adapted to pronouns. His tricks were to sit, shake, lie down, and roll over, only he had greedily come to a place where if you had a treat, he threw his paw up and did the whole routine at once. In a neighborhood demonstration, I said that it wasn't the tone of voice, as someone had suggested, but the actual words that Smoky understood, and to prove this, I let the paperboy get a block away on his bicycle and then in a sweet singsong voice said: *Get him, Smoky.*

And he did, though thankfully without teeth involved. He knocked the boy from his bike and stood there waiting for whatever was coming next. What came next is that I got in trouble and Smoky was no longer allowed to run loose but had to be on a chain while the backyard got fenced in. He was a one-family dog, and visitors knew not to make quick moves or raise their voices. In fact, my sister and I successfully terrorized a cousin who was babysitting by simply asking the dog to *watch her* and *stay.* I am not proud of having done this, our cousin standing up on a chair for a long time while we ate ice cream and did as we pleased, but we were always very proud of Smoky and how smart he was and how devoted he was to us, his family, as we were to him. In fact, when I went to camp, I got letters from him, something my dad continued when my sister went off to college and then when I did as well.

Smoky did all kinds of things in these letters, stories we loved to tell, especially to my grandmother, who was entering dementia. We told how he went off to school but got kicked out for smoking pot. We told her he had a black leather jacket and rode a motorcycle. *Hush*, she said. *I hope he has a helmet.* And then a moment later she asked if that was a true story or a joke. If we didn't offer her these tales, she asked for them. For the most part the stories were tall tales, but there really was the time he bit and tore a woman's pants (she came into that fenced-in yard uninvited), and when the insurance adjuster showed up for what my dad referred to as his mug shot, Smoky rolled onto his back and lay sprawled there in the most submissive pose possible.

In the years after Smoky died, my dad would swear that he saw him from time to time there in the backyard, especially around dusk and early evening while he was grilling or just sitting on the back step to smoke his pipe. My mom suggested one beer too many, but the power of suggestion was great and there was a way the shadows hung over where Smoky's house had been that did indeed look like he was there. The Smoky stories then evolved into Smoky sightings, this dog delivered by prayer, something my parents mentioned often over the years, the word *manipulation* often woven into the mix.

Flash forward about eighteen years after his death, to when my son was around seven and going through what we now refer to as his existential phase, a time when he thought a lot about death (he called it "my fear") and had trouble sleeping. Other than his *fear,* it was a time when he was obsessed with Pokémon, the Red Sox, and boycotting Hebrew School. He and his older sister spent a lot of time playing with our two dogs: a sweet, plump yellow Labrador named Vanessa (named for Vanessa Williams, whom my son had a crush on) and Daisy, an oversized sheltie who was devoted to making the kids be where she thought they *should* be, a practice she wearily continued well into their teenage years.

During some sessions with a doctor who was helping my son get over the fear, he was asked what he would say if suddenly granted with three wishes. He wished: (1) to live a normal life plus one hundred years, (2) that the people he loves would live a normal life plus a hundred years, and (3) a papillon.

A papillon? He wanted a papillon, his hands going up to imitate the large butterfly ears. It seemed an easy enough wish to grant in light of it all. The fear, after all, had originated with the loss of his grandfathers and the many questions he had about how and why and *what happens then?* For his second wish to be such a generous one, it seemed only right that the generosity be returned, except that no one I spoke to who had in possession these tiny delicate creatures thought that a household with two young children, a Lab, and a sheltie was a good fit. And so we went in search of the answer. I realize now that the pet-store purchase broke all kinds of ethical codes, but I didn't know it at the time and simply continued a routine we had long had of going to this one place to look and see and sometimes sit on the floor and play with puppies. My children ran from cage to cage, falling in love with first one and then another. His sister wanted them all, already thinking of names and thinking of how she would dress them as she had sweet Vanessa, who was often found in teen-heartthrob or camp T-shirts and socks, lounging on the sofa. But my son could think only of papillons, and all of a sudden, he was pointing to a cage and a little black ball of fur and saying, *There's one!*

The woman who worked there was at his side in seconds, affirming his identification. "Not full-blooded," she said, and with her hands on his shoulders gently pushed him closer to the pen covered with cedar shavings. "But there is definitely some papillon in there." I knew this wasn't true and maybe his sister knew as well, but we were all willing to let imagination and wish fulfillment take over at that point. Wasn't it enough simply to believe? Like Dumbo with his feather or the children in *Peter Pan* with their fairy dust?

"His name is Buster," his sister announced. "Buster Boo," though over the years he took on other nicknames. At Bennington College, where I teach and am on campus twice a year in a house with other faculty members who bring their dogs (the Dog House), he was sometimes, in his earlier years, referred to as Lil Hef, a playboy especially attracted to a large voluptuous Lab who had no idea he was back there making his moves. At home, he was known as my shadow, and his most affectionate pet name was Boolie.

Part Shih Tzu and part poodle and perhaps something else, Boolie was a scruffy little twelve-pound dust mop who thought he was much bigger than he was; his ears did not stand up high like a butterfly but flopped down like his Beatle-style haircut and Dr. Seuss–looking tail. Still, we called him our papillon and did for fifteen years. If you came into our house there at the end, you would have seen this elderly little guy with a gray goatee in a blue argyle sweater curled on a blanket or my pillow and snoring like a truck driver. He was deaf except for the highest-pitched whistles, and his vision was fading fast. He followed me from room to room, as he had done for years, waiting on my pillow if I wasn't home, but in those final days, if I got up to leave the room, he would give an exasperated sigh. I tried my best to teach him *I'll be right back*, but he never understood this and continued to get up and follow.

Before he died, I had no idea how much I talked all day long in the plural. *Let's take a break now*, I would say. Or *Time for lunch!* Or I read things aloud and he simply listened or dozed through them. I felt as I had years before with the loss of Smoky, and in the same way, I kept thinking I saw him on the foot of the bed, or perched in the window. I heard the jingling of his tags or felt him flop down near my feet. He was a symbol of long life and of the universal wish for immortality. And like Smoky, he had appeared at just the right time—the answer to a prayer, a wish granted—to instill faith and trust in the purest form of unconditional love.

*Teresa Miller met Scout three years ago, when
Scout, a kitten at the time, hitched a ride on
Teresa's car. Their journey continues.*

The One-Eyed Dog

TERESA MILLER

A friend asked me, "Why write about Tuffy? It's not as if he pulled a fake Lassie and saved you from an abandoned well, an old mine shaft, or some other dark hole." Except he did.

IN SPITE OF our loss, I was normal enough to have wanted a doll or even a cowgirl hat, but my grandmother had bought me a cedar trunk, so we could keep my mother's memory alive. Sort of. For just to be clear, this was no ordinary hope chest, filled with delicate linens set aside for happier days. Instead, it was overflowing with old report cards, diplomas, and autograph books, some with giddy inscriptions about how bright the future would be.

There was also the rusty harmonica and Grandma's attached note: *Your mother worked after school to buy what she called a French harp.* But she'd never gotten around to actually playing it before she smelled of cedar, and then we were rummaging through what might have been.

My mother had died after giving birth to my brother, and Grandma had kept her bright red maternity jacket, too. I still have it, along with Grandma's full-out missive, trying to make sense of it all before settling on this: *God loved her so much he called her home.* Not that it matters, but maybe it does—she'd written it on letterhead from my grandfather's furniture store and folded it into a Bible.

Did I mention I was only two when Mother died, that this trunk didn't come along until later, after I was able to kneel beside it all on my own? Still, it's where my memories begin—with those secret drawers at Grandma's house. And, oh yes, some dime-store jewelry, already starting to fade. Think plastic turquoise. "Priceless," Grandma said.

I understand better now—the trunk became her strongbox of grief. It was just different for me, especially after I found a baby book alongside the funeral roster. For Mother had overcome her own frailties to record my first words, a mantra really for living without her: our family names, *moon, splash*, and *Tuffy*.

Tuffy was my mother's dog, her legacy to me, and though there were still everyday reminders of what we'd lost—Mother's kitchen clock had started to buzz—Tuffy was clearly of this world, shaped in part by the gentleness that had left it. If he raised his paw when you extended a hand, it was because my mother had taught him to do so. If he sat when you asked him to roll over, well... She'd taught him the difference, only to indulge him if he'd had other ideas.

As for the rest of his backstory, it was sketchy and mainly came from Grandma, who claimed she didn't like dogs and stuck to the basics. Apparently, Mother had found a litter of part-terrier, all-mongrel pups on the college campus, where she worked in the business office. Her fear was that they'd wind up in the science lab, so she'd secured homes for all of them but Tuffy, reportedly saying, "He's so ugly he's cute."

This was the closest we ever came to laughing about Mother—or even Tuffy, whose name had clearly set him up for some serious karma. Mother herself had nursed him through a severe case of mange, and then shortly after her death, he'd gotten hit by a car and lost an eye. The vet had recommended mercy, but my father wouldn't have it. He said, "Not after everything." So Tuffy had earned his pedigree by becoming the only one-eyed dog in Tahlequah, Oklahoma, circa 1956.

I have before and after pictures. The first is from my christening day. Mother and I are all dressed up on the front porch, where I appear comfortable in her arms. But I'm reaching out to Tuffy, who has both eyes trained on someone beyond us. A finger shadow. My grandmother? My dad? The other photo's more of a blur, my brother Mark, bundled against the cold to stand with Tuffy. His hand's gotten big enough to hide Tuffy's scar.

No captions necessary. We all knew what was missing. The trick was to salvage what we could, and that's where Tuffy came in. He smelled of sunshine, fresh air, and children.

So in the beginning, Mark and I followed him, just never outside the neighborhood. For he seemed to understand boundaries, even as he taught us to dig up the roses, Grandpa's gift, roped off in the backyard. We were good at it, the digging that is, molding ourselves to the earth, sniffing the world around us, and letting the days collect beneath our fingernails.

We also learned to hunt for a different kind of quarry, treeing squirrels or chasing rabbits, just to capture a moment. No need for Dr. Phil here. We wanted to feel spared, too. One squirrel even took to chasing us, bringing us closer to that instant when we'd collapse with laughter, Tuffy right beside us, his non-eye twitching with all he couldn't see. "Roll over," we'd say, and he'd nudge us with his nose.

And the best? Sometimes we'd catch a glimpse of the moon in broad daylight and dust ourselves off to greet it. The science isn't there yet, but somehow this was Tuffy's doing.

It's worth noting we were largely unsupervised, partly due to the false security that comes from thinking the worst has already happened.

Also, we knew virtually everyone, so to play off a more familiar theory, it took a village, a distracted housekeeper, and a dog to raise us.

But then one afternoon, a man we didn't recognize pulled his black sedan onto the fringes of the yard, propping open the door and calling out that our father had sent him—he needed us down at the law office. Insert *naïveté*. We'd never actually been told not to get into a car with strangers, since we'd never really met any. So we were all set to go until Tuffy bounded forward, his white fur bristling as he stationed himself between the car and us. There was only a brief standoff before the man screeched into the distance. And word spread, once we ran inside, terrified after the fact—the one-eyed dog had stared him down.

Of course, this led to all sorts of speculation about the man's motives, but he'd disappeared, leaving Grandma to join others in saying, "We'll never know." But she wasn't just talking about him. She'd brought me over a telescope for my ninth birthday, and we set in up in the backyard one night. Tuffy himself pressed against me as I tilted it toward the sky.

"You don't really need a telescope to see the moon," my father said, staring up at it on his own.

Except sometimes you did.

———— ҩ ————

My father had married, divorced, and married again. Grandma had taken up cryptograms, reminding everyone that *y* could sometimes be *r*. And Grandpa, usually on the down low, had begun planting and replanting roses all over town.

Somehow the changes became more real after friends gave us another dog and Tuffy started following us. Not that he seemed to feel slighted at all. For even with Tippy in tow, he enjoyed our outings as much as we did—joining in as we staked out the park across the street and built rock bridges through the creek. Occasionally, we'd lose our footing, splashing him as we slipped into the shallow water, but he'd just shake off the deluge, splashing us back.

Then a little later, as my stepmother settled in, he began coming to school. I first spotted him looking in the window of our fifth-grade classroom. We'd been studying our *Weekly Readers*, casting our minds across the waters to ask if kids in Russia ate TV dinners. And there he was, his paw raised as if to shake hands with the entire class. "That's Tuffy," I shouted, coming into my own, for I'd heard all the whispered speculations about our family, mundane things about who packed our lunches and got the holidays cards we crafted in class. But nothing in their imaginations or the *Reader* itself could compete with the wonder of a one-eyed dog.

He visited routinely after that, once even slipping into the hallway before the principal shooed him outside.

His defining journey, though, didn't come until after we left on a trip to meet my stepmother's family in Chicago. We'd hired someone to watch over the dogs, as if there were some sort of transaction for leaving love behind. It didn't work, not for the dogs anyway. They'd turned up at Grandpa's store for the first time ever, crossing a busy highway, Tuffy in the lead as they searched for us. My grandmother, the one who didn't like dogs, found peculiar validation in this—Tuffy knew.

In fact, he almost knew too much and became restless over the next few years as we grew beyond him. He didn't get my new transistor radio. He didn't get the Beatles. Mostly he didn't get a twelve-year-old girl, who could bypass a baby possum to jump in with a carload of friends. One spring morning he even tugged at me, more demanding than usual as I rushed off to school. So I paused just long enough to brush my hand across his scar, and then he let me go.

It was that night he went missing in a way that immediately frightened us. He'd always been a free-range dog—pretty much the custom in those days, especially in small towns. Still, he never ventured far from us, and so we tracked him by tracking ourselves. We checked the park, the school, the furniture store, and, with increasing dread, all the busy intersections. But a neighbor tipped us off. She'd seen him earlier with a pack of dogs, and we knew then—how need had led us all astray. Tuffy was gone, even before he returned to us, mortally wounded by a wildness that was alien to him.

I couldn't bear to look at him, but I did. Over and over, because the images stayed with me—they woke me in the middle of the night; they ambushed me on the playground; they followed me to Grandma's house.

This was the bond I shared with Mark. We both longed for a gentler scenario and built a fountain in Tuffy's memory, beneath the shade of a sugar maple, one of his favorite spots on summer days. We vowed to preserve it, but… After a while it became a haven for squirrels, rabbits, birds—new life.

All of which is to say that grief, love, and joy can be free-range, too, and I've wandered through the years. I gave Mother's harmonica to a man I loved and two decades later asked for it back. I added Grandma's blue beads to the cedar chest—they match the old turquoise better than you'd think. And I've even hunted down some final words for Tuffy, not to put him to rest but to set him free: *He's survived by the moon, acres of wild roses, and his children.*

JILL MOMADAY

N. Scott Momaday pauses from an artwork in progress to pose with his "granddog," Chino. Momaday follows in his parents' footsteps: his mother was a writer and his father a painter.

The Bear

N. SCOTT MOMADAY

What ruse of vision
escarping the wall of leaves,
    rending incision
into countless surfaces,

    would cull and color
his somnolence, whose old age
    has outworn valor,
all but the fact of courage?

    Seen, he does not come,
move, but seems forever there,
    dimensionless, dumb,
in the windless noon's hot glare.

    More scarred than others
these years since the trap maimed him,
    pain slants his withers,
drawing up the crooked limb.

    Then he is gone, whole,
without urgency, from sight,
    as buzzards control,
imperceptibly, their flight.

On the Neva

He waits, who describes rainbows.
Then more than the morning wind
Strums the beaded string.
He sets himself, sturdy on the plane of ice.
Nearly numb, his hands tease and turn
The frantic creature into the circle below him
And suddenly heave it into sight,
And when it strikes the air
It freezes instantly and becomes iridescent,
And traces a perfect arc across
The soft and smoking sun.

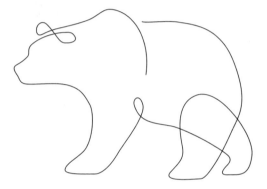

Joyce Carol Oates and Cherie balance work and play together, as chronicled frequently on Joyce's Twitter account (@JoyceCarolOates).

Photograph by © LAURA PEDRICK

JUBILATE: An Homage in Catterel* Verse

JOYCE CAROL OATES

For I will consider my Cat Cherie

for she is the very apotheosis of Cat-Beauty

which is to say, nothing extraordinary

for in the Cat, beauty *is* ordinary

like the bliss

conferred

upon us

in the hypnosis

of purr-

ing.

She has been known

to knead her claws

upon a sleeve.

And on a knee.

And on bare skin,

sharp claws sinking in—

just a warning.

* "Catterel"—an elevated variant of "doggerel"

For she is of the *tribe of Tyger*
and eyes *burning bright*
though cuddling
at night
until you wake to discover—
where is she? *Cher-ie?*
Don't inquire.

     ***

For in considering my Cat Cherie
I am considering Catitude—
each Cat the (essential)
equivalent of all others
not varying freak-
ishly in size
(like crude D*gs)
but pleas-
ingly Platonic.
Cat-chutzpah
is the "sheathed
claw"—
no heart borne
upon a foreleg,
but
your challenge
to decode,
like poetry
of a subtlety
that *does not bark*
its meaning

but forces us to
be just a little
smarter than
we are.
(Unlike D*gs
whose un-
critical adulation
makes us
dumber.)
　　　***
Of Twitter it is estimated
somewhere beyond thirty-one percent
who tweet are feline,
in nocturnal prowl
slyly retweeting
their kind,
reproducing,
replicating
the dark rapacious ever-
fecund *feral-soul*
that is the sea
upon which "civilization"
floats, uneasily.
For such eloquent Kitty-Twitter,
only the most elegant Kitty-Litter.
But if you ask—*Cherie, what*
is this? the reply is
blank blinking innocence.
Mew? What's with you?

***

--"Live free
or die"—is the Cat's
very soul, that
makes of us,
by contrast,
fawning and obsequious
beings (not unlike
D*gs). Such beauty
instructs us in its own
perfection
for it is beyond
mere "use"—no *work-*
cats, watch-cats,
plebeian beings
but each descended
of gods
as ancient Egypt
honored; and how
like a deity, to sink
teeth into a rat,
a creature that
squeamish
mankind abhors,
while maintaining
purest Cat-
innocence.

***

Sandpaper tongue,

utter long

-ing.

Cat-love the nudge

of furry-hard head.

But oh, where has she gone?

Kitty-kitty-*kitty!* She may come

when called

(like the D*g)

but mostly

she will not

for

(unlike the D*g),

she has got

an interior life,

inscrutable,

inaccessible,

un-possessable.

She does not aim

to please, or aim

at all. Her blessing

is a fluke, as readily

withdrawn as given.

Never will she *do your bidding.*

Never will she falsely flatter,

nor deceive you

that you much matter

beyond the reach

of the hand that pets

and feeds.

Also she has got
much busyness
out-of-doors
by moonlight.
Don't inquire.

      ***

But there she has gone
head-first through
the Plexiglas cat-door
to return with,
dropped on the floor
at my feet,
a small carcass very still.
Oh Cherie, what have you done?

      ***

Only the Cat's gift is freely given.
The D*g in subservience as in chains
has no free will, and so—
Oh Cherie—is this for me?

      ***

For I will consider my Cat Cherie
whose tail switches irritably
across these keys
when confronted with prose
found wanting.
For it is irrefutable, the Cat
is the harshest critic of prose, cattedly
rejecting what has been doggedly
written.

This will not do, at all.
This is not it. At all
where the D*g drools
delight with very mediocrity,
in complicity.
Sometimes, the furry Cat-
sprawl
obliterates the typescript
utterly
for you dare not move
a limb, a tail—
even (gingerly)
from the laptop—
at risk
of provoking a hiss—
Mew! Whom're you touching, you!
     ***

If I dare rise
from this desk
prematurely—
if I dare plead
(human) exhaustion--
vehemently
Cherie will dig in her claws
securing my knees
with the cry *Mew!*
Where d'you think you're going, you!
Thus hours, days & ages
accumulate in pages

and pages into books
and books into *oeuvres*.
Purrlific the literary
judgment.

***

The very best books (it is said)
are not *ghost-* but *cat-*written.
Simenon, Colette, John le Carré
not least Hemingway—
Auden, Eliot, Philip K. Dick—
Borges and Burroughs and
Patricia Highsmith—
Jean Cocteau and Henry David Thoreau—
H. P. Lovecraft and Edgar Allan Poe—
 ("I wish I could write as mysterious as a cat!")--
Twain, Bradbury, Raymond Chandler—
Sartre, Sylvia Plath, and—Daniel Handler?—
not least Samuel Johnson—
("But Hodge shan't be shot; no, no Hodge
shall not be shot")—
rapidly retreating into the mists of Time
where Muse is suffused with Mouse
until the two are merged in mystery—
Cat and collaborator.

AUTHOR'S NOTE: This is based upon Christopher Smart's great poem "For I Will Consider My Cat Jeoffry." —J. C. O.

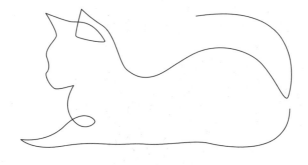

Susan Orlean discovered her love for donkeys on a trip to
Fez, Morocco, and has carried it with her ever since. Animals
make frequent appearances in her writing.

Photograph by © COREY HENDRICKSON

Dog Memory

SUSAN ORLEAN

W H A T   I   N O T I C E the most is the sound, or rather the absence
of sounds: I miss the click of Cooper's nails on the wooden floor,
the jingling of his tags (so exasperating at times that we considered
buying those rubber jingle-stoppers). And because he was an itchy
dog, there was often the drum major's *thump-thump-thump* as Cooper
worked his back leg up and down to scratch behind his ear. There
was the requisite announcement of the mailman's arrival and the
parading of other dogs on the sidewalk in front of our house (how
dare they!), and in the evening, after a good walk and supper, there
was the gummy munching when he was busy with a bully stick.
Cooper was a symphony of a sort, and I know I will experience
phantom dog noises for a while.

Cooper, my good boy, my Welsh springer spaniel, died unexpectedly
last weekend at the age of nine. It happened when we were away from
home, so his death felt very abstract until we got back last night. This
morning I thought I heard him stirring in his bed, but it was just the
window shade, shifting in a bit of breeze. My ear kept searching for his
other signature noises, and found only stillness instead.

If therapists didn't charge you and were willing to chase sticks, they
would be dogs. The kindly and receptive silence, the respect for secrets,
the inexhaustible supply of attention—these are a dog's, and a therapist's,
finest qualities. Dogs, though, are more fun than therapists—more
tender, more dear, more doting, and certainly more admiring.

Over the last nine years, I've written a lot of stories and even a book about animals. Given the endless number of interesting stories there are in the world, I've sometimes wondered how I ended up on this particular path, choosing these particular stories, so rich with critters. Certainly, I've always loved animals, and they are also an ideal foil for examining the human condition; it all started, though, when I got Cooper, nine years ago, after a long, dog-less decade. I had gotten my first dog when I was in college, and we were best friends and stalwart companions. Her death, thirteen years later, from cancer was horribly drawn out and deeply sad, and I didn't think I had the stomach to go through having—and losing—a dog ever again. But of course I wanted one, and when I finally got Cooper, a lovely freckle-faced beast, the subject of animals—living with them, loving them, hoarding them, using them, and how our relationship to animals says something about who and what we are—was stirred up for me, and I wanted to write about them again and again. I'm glad of that. I will certainly not go another decade without a dog, because now I know that even though dogs break your heart, they fill it up, even when they're gone.

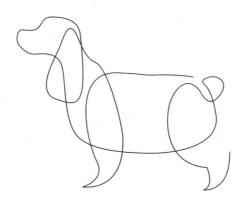

PATRICIA PADGETT

Ron Padgett and Susie, circa 1978. Susie was featured in one of Ron's poems, "Lost and Found."

Animals and Art

RON PADGETT

I WAS SAYING that sometimes I feel sorry for wild animals, out there in the dark, looking for something to eat while in fear of being eaten. And they have no ballet companies or art museums. Animals of course are not aware of their lack of cultural activities, and therefore do not regret their absence. I was saying this to my wife as we walked along a path in the woods. Every once in a while she would go Unh-huh or Hmmm, but I suspected that she was wondering why I was saying such things. I was saying them in order to see how they would feel when spoken without any hint of irony. Then I quoted the remark about human life as nasty, brutish, and short, but neither she nor I could recall who had said that, though I offered a guess. In fact I had seen the quotation ascribed to someone recently, but I did not mention this to her, for fear of appearing senile. But the truth is that I do not bother to try to remember information that I can look up in a reference book, thinking, I suppose, that I would prefer to fill my mind with the impressions and sensations and spontaneous ideas and mental images that fly past so quickly. Would such a person as I make a good animal? The news today is that scientists have finished the genetic mapping of the human being, and it turns out that we are 99 per cent chimpanzee. I don't feel 99 per cent chimpanzee.

It makes me wonder about the enormity of the remaining one per cent, the sliver that causes me to take the subway up to the Met and look at pictures and sculptures and other beautiful and interesting objects, then go to the museum cafeteria and have a cup of tea and a bun, all without the fear that some creature is going to eat me. But back of all of it is a spreading sorrow for those that hide and tremble in the dark.

Elise Paschen sits beside her golden retrievers Charlie and Chai, while holding her cat Tiger Lily. In her life as in her poetry, animal and human relationships thrive.

JOE McCUNE

Prey

ELISE PASCHEN

If my daughter observes the paperback
splayed on the floor beside the barricade

of laundry hampers, wicker baskets, pillows
stuffing the gaps, she will discern I was

the one who hurled the book into the jaws
of 4 a.m., protective of my shrinking

threshold, confounded by feline affection,
attempting to silence the yowling cat

during the hours when sleep escapes, because
his sense of self is fierce, because he cudgels

our bedroom door, because deep down I love
a dog. How throughout each day the cat's paws

battle beneath the study door, how afterwards
he leaps to the armchair beside the desk

green eyes ablaze, long whiskers twitching, striped
fluffed-up tail thumping, full-bellied white heaving.

O Tiger Lily of Pawhuska, orphaned
barn kitten who adopted our young daughter

the day we buried deep my father's ashes:
Do not betray my confidence. Don't let

our daughter know I threw the *William Blake*
against the floor to frighten you away,

to stop you clawing into the dark thicket
of night before the birds, your prey, catch fire.

Quarrel of Sparrows

When I take flight
far from the house—

        lonely for choirs,
        riotous in trees—

a visitation
of wings, whirs, arcs

        in sky, then lights
        on city sidewalk.

How they survive
winter, back-alley

        scrappers, who worry
        feeders for millet,

sunflower seeds,
bicker for hours,

        while my boots plod
        across brick driveway

in January,
crunching the snow.

        I track the bright
        dash of their chatter,

while the crisscrossing
of wings will shadow

across my day
into the night,

such brazen pluck
soldiering the storm.

Adrift in the house,
we'll sleep while staunch

house sparrows huddle
together guarded

against the white.
Flurries inside—

their fury dies.
The snow won't stop.

Photograph by © JOANNE S. LAWTON / WASHINGTON BUSINESS JOURNAL

Diane Rehm and her late dog Maxie used to spend time in the studio together. Diane's third memoir, Life with Maxie, *chronicles the impact of a special pet.*

The Emperor Maxie

DIANE REHM

WHEN I WATCHED the living creature I had so deeply loved
for more than fourteen years let go of life, I was honored to realize he
trusted me so much that he chose to die in my arms, breathing his last
breath, letting his head fall over, all the while nestled in my lap.

Maxie was a long-haired Chihuahua, a beautiful boy named for the
Emperor Maximilian and given his less-than-imperial nickname on the
day we brought him home. However, except for his interactions with
me, his primary caregiver, Maxie was not what those he took a bite
out of during his lifetime would call a friendly dog. In fact, I dare not
recall the names of all the people in Washington, DC, Maxie was either
hostile to or actually bit, even as a small puppy.

I, as his adoring companion, attributed his unfriendly disposition
to the fact that Maxie had been held and fondled as a tiny pup by two
young children who had rushed to our home expressly to see him. They
scooped him out of my arms, snuggled to hug and kiss him, and then,
as he wriggled to free himself, let him fall onto a hard wood floor, right
on his head. It was after that fall that the biting and hostility began,
his trust given only to me and, after a long while, to my late husband,
John Rehm.

John himself wasn't quite ready for a puppy. He had asked me
to wait until I "retired" before thinking of taking on a new dog.
However, after our beloved and beautiful long-haired red dachshund,
Katinka, died several years earlier at age fifteen, I'd never quite been

able to fill the void she left in my life. She'd been bred once, but I wasn't ready to take on more than one dog, so her entire litter was distributed to caring households in the area. And besides, I said to John, I had no intention of retiring.

One summer day while I was on vacation at our home, as John and I sat having a leisurely breakfast, I decided to wander through the "for sale" ads in the *Washington Post*. And there, lo and behold, was the very dog I'd been looking and longing for since John and I had first laid eyes on a long-haired Chihuahua at the Dallas airport.

I admit, I fell head over heels in love with that dog's beautiful face, his long hair and gentleness, as he lay in his owner's lap having his tummy stroked. She allowed me to pet the dog and even to play with his paws, as he happily batted my hand back and forth. I had thought about that creature for months and months, until finally, there was the ad.

I immediately dialed the number listed and made an appointment with the breeder, while John continued to remind me of my promise to wait until I retired before getting a dog. But after arranging to meet the breeder that very morning, I responded to John by saying, "I just want to look. Surely no harm in *looking.*" Reluctantly, he got into the car with me as we drove to a real estate office in the suburbs. And there, on the carpeted floor, were not one but *two* adorable black long-haired Chihuahuas. In my moment of exuberance and excitement, I said, "I'll take *both* of them!" I wanted to scoop up both the male and the female, take them in my arms, and run out the door with them to the car. But after a long and, at moments, rather tense discussion with John, we both agreed that one pup would be enough, and, together, we chose Maxie.

He was a smart pup, learning quickly the rules of the house, the difference between the garden, where he was encouraged to respond to his bodily needs, and the kitchen, where he stayed for the first few weeks of his life. Before long, he was sleeping in our bed, with just a bit of a challenge: Maxie would not allow John to get into the bed with me! He began to growl and threaten John! It took lots of persuading, cajoling, and peacemaking to end the standoff, but we were finally able to become a comfortable and compatible threesome. I must say John's patience wore thin at times, and I didn't blame him. But who of us would want to make a choice between an adored puppy and a beloved husband?

While we lived in a four-story home with a large garden for the first seven years of his life, Maxie had the run of the garden, playfully racing up and down the long fence with the dog next door, sitting with me as I worked in the garden, or retrieving a toy as we played with him on our patio. But the time came when we were forced to move to a condominium because my husband had developed Parkinson's disease. We needed a one-story dwelling and were fortunate enough to find a beautiful place overlooking acres of park and trees.

Of course, that meant a huge adjustment in Maxie's regimen, since he'd never learned to walk on a leash. It took quite a bit of persuading, but he finally got used to the idea that soft grass and beautiful trees were a little farther away than just outside the back door.

Parkinson's disease eventually forced my husband and me to make the sad decision to move him out of our wonderful condo and into a nursing home, where he could have round-the-clock care. Fortunately, it was a facility that allowed, indeed welcomed, pets. Some residents even had their pets living with them. But Maxie just became a regular visitor, joining me each day as I went from work, where Maxie kept me company in my office, to the nursing home, for a daily visit with John.

Maxie was happy to lick John's face and then lie at the foot of his bed as my husband and I chatted away through the afternoons.

At some point during that time, Maxie began to develop a cough, mild at first but which over some months became increasingly severe. After many tests, veterinarians determined that he had respiratory heart disease as well as a thinning of the bronchial passages, which was limiting his ability to get enough air into his lungs and causing the cough. There was specialized medication prescribed, but still, the worrisome cough became more intense as time went on.

On the night of June 22, 2014, it was clear that my beloved husband's life was coming to an end. So Maxie and I stayed at the nursing facility, putting two chairs together, trying to create what turned out to be a most uncomfortable bed. Maxie was on my stomach until, at two a.m., I gave up. Actually, I got up and began writing what ultimately became my book *On My Own,* while Maxie slept. John died at ten o'clock the next morning.

Maxie and I lived by ourselves in my condominium for the next two years, as his chronic coughing intensified. The veterinarians could do nothing more. Maxie slept more and more, moved more slowly, but continued eating well. Inevitably, an evening came, in December 2016, when he could not stop coughing. I thought perhaps fresh air might help, so I put on his leash and carried him downstairs, hoping to take him for a short walk. Instead, when I put him on the ground, he did something he'd never done before: He simply sat down and looked at me.

I picked Maxie up, took him to my car, and, with him nestled on a blanket in my lap, drove as quickly as I could to the vet's. Now, I must tell you, Maxie *hated* going to the vet's. He had to be muzzled each time he was examined to prevent him from biting the clinicians or the doctors. Nevertheless, I felt I had to take him there, hoping they might be able to do something to help him.

Instead, just as we drove into the garage of the vet's office building, my darling Maxie, that wise little ten-pound pup, looked up at me one last time, and right then and there, in my lap, in my arms, in our car, even before I turned the engine off, took his last breath.

Even so, I rushed him upstairs to the vet's office, where a technician took one look, grabbed him from me and ran back to the treatment area. He placed him on a table, where he was immediately surrounded by three vets, who put their hands on him, ready to revive him if they could. But I yelled, "Stop! Let him go!" and watched as they all abruptly raised their arms. Maxie was gone.

Maxie was one of the great loves of my life, not a perfect pup by any estimation. Love can be—and always is—accepting and understanding the less-than-perfect behaviors of another creature, animal or otherwise.

JAY WATSON

Jewell Parker Rhodes shares her life with two toy sheepdogs, Ripley and Gurgi. Here, she writes about her one and only cat, Griffin.

Griffin

JEWELL PARKER RHODES

She wasn't supposed to be my cat.

My daughter, ten, brought home a kitten—tiny, fierce, and darkest black with streaks of grey and brown.

"Griffin." Accent on *"grif"* with a rolling, high pitch, then with a lower timbre, *"fin."*

"Griffin."

Griffin was adopted too young. Feral, she bit and scratched, drawing blood. Her yellow eyes, almond-shaped, dared anyone to touch her.

One, two, three, four years of gentleness, soft murmurs, instructing, "No bites." Finally, she tolerated caresses—but only on her head.

Just eight pounds, Griffin stalked like a lion and eagle. A Jack Russell Terrier and two cats were no match for her. She strutted like a general and the animals parted before her, paying homage to her intensity.

"Griffin."

Never once did she cry or meow. Her mouth would open, close. Open, close. No sound.

I fed Griffin—morning and night—but she wasn't my cat.

Mute, she observed the children playing, me writing tales, and the birds outside. Inside, she hunted scorpions.

She wasn't my cat.

Griffin opened doors. Flinging her body upwards, her front paws downward on the latch, Griffin roamed where she pleased. She couldn't be kept out.

The Jack Russell died, then one cat, then another. My daughter went to college, married, gave birth to a daughter. She rescued a kitten then, a special-needs cat.

Griffin was never my cat.

Yet, as she aged, Griffin spent days languidly following me from room to room. Or else lying on my desk while I typed on my computer. Still, she didn't talk. Just watched. Claiming her right to be by my side.

I didn't like cats (not ever).

Griffin became mine.

I patted her head, my hand stroking to the tip of her tail. She didn't scratch or bite; instead, her eyes blinked. Occasionally, her voice box trembled. Still no "meow," but a soft, quiet purr.

She wasn't my cat. I preferred dogs. I adopted two toy Australian Sheepdogs. Even as puppies, they treated Griffin with the awe and respect due an Empress Cat.

Griffin belonged to my daughter who left long ago.

Eyes aglow, Griffin watched the puppies grow—licking and pawing for petting and belly rubs. She watched them hop, clamber on the bed, and sleep next to me. She envied them playing outside.

Griffin decided to speak "dog."

She licked my hand and face, her tongue like sandpaper. She let me cradle her, carrying her weaker self from room to room.

With a single nail, she poked me. Her version of pawing for attention. *Poke. Poke. Poke.* She let me touch her belly.

She slept on the bed. Not in the middle, snuggling on sheets with the pack-loving dogs. She slept on the pillow, beside my head, where I could feel and hear her chest rising and falling.

"Night, Griffin."

Sunny afternoons, I let her outside with the dogs. "Coyotes," I'd say and, amazingly, she understood me and never left the yard. Sometimes she lay on the pet trampoline, sphinx-like, watching the dogs run and play-growl.

Griffin was my elder, elderly cat. The dogs would bark their emotions. Happy, hungry, restless. Griffin's mouth opened, a small "o," her long whiskers flickering, and she made an "Ack" sound. "Ack." Not a meow, just "Ack." She demanded more focused attention.

It was clear that Griffin, from her newfound behaviors, had chosen me. She was my cat. I loved her guiding, telling me how to better show my love. I did love her. Griffin had melted my heart years ago.

She was my cat.

Griffin was dying, her lungs filling with fluid. I held her, touched my head to her tiny body. She purred and purred. A definite "I love you" sound.

She drew her last breath … her eyes glazing, then becoming thick and still.

Griffin was my best and only cat.

Wade Rouse (left) and his husband, Gary Edwards,
stand on the steps of their cottage in Michigan,
known as "Turkey Run," with their dogs Mabel (on
the steps) and Doris.

HAYDEN STINEBAUGH

Christmas Cookie

WADE ROUSE

"NO!" I SAID to my husband, Gary, and then to the dog he was holding in his lap. "I'm leaving!"

I was standing in an animal shelter just before Christmas. Gary had brought me here as a surprise, telling me he'd found the perfect gift for his parents. I expected it to be a Yankee Candle, not a black Lab mix.

"I'm not going to be part of this scheme, Lucy," I continued. "Your parents are too overwhelmed for us to spring a dog on them, much less now."

Gary's father had just been diagnosed with Parkinson's, and the news had hit him hard. He'd recently retired, and his dreams of a perfect, peaceful sojourn into old age seemed quashed. Moreover, Gary's mother seemed overwhelmed by the news, too, unable to focus or find peace.

Gary held the dog up, waved its arms, and made it act as if it were talking to me, just like he did with our rescue, Marge, whom we'd adopted from this same shelter.

"Save me," Gary said in a falsetto, his head hidden behind the dog's.

Gary lowered the Lab into his lap, kissed her on top of her head, and then looked at me. "Help me save my parents," he said, his voice suddenly emotional, his eyes brimming with tears.

I had always been told the worst holiday gift you could get someone was a pet, because the cuteness would wear off as soon as Christmas turned to the dead of winter. And acquiring a pet was not a decision someone else made for you.

"Do your parents even want a dog?" I asked. "Don't they have enough to deal with already?"

"They *need* this dog," Gary said, trying not to cry. "They *need* a little joy and happiness. They *need* to focus on something full of life." He stopped and nodded at her papers, which were sitting beside him on the floor. "And her name is Cookie. Could there be a better sign? Christmas Cookie."

I looked out the window of the shelter, the word *need* running through my head.

I thought of my mom, a hospice nurse and longtime animal advocate, who firmly believed that two things could save nearly any soul: prayer and penicillin. Our Ozarks home on ten acres of woods was often a dumping ground for stray cats and dogs, and my mom would try to bring back to life each and every broken body, bone, soul, and spirit she came across. She would suture and sooth kittens, and old hurt hounds, before setting off in search of the perfect home for them.

There was never "a right time" for her to help a lost animal or soul. She headed out at all times, day or night, because these animals needed help. My family ended up with a menagerie of dogs and cats who became my support system—my best friends, my confidants— as a gay kid growing up in the middle of the Ozarks. I needed them, all of them.

I thought of Marge, the eighty-five-pound rescue mutt we adopted in the same place we were now. Marge—the puppy we saved after she was dumped in the city and left to die—was the dog I didn't want or need either. But Marge was the one who got me back on my feet and moving again, the one who helped me lose nearly 100 pounds. She was the one who coaxed me through numerous books, without ever leaving my feet for a single second. Without Gary and without Marge, I wouldn't have finished a single book, nor would I have learned to embrace life and love again without fear paralyzing me.

I am a writer. My world is both very large but also very small. It is hard to let people into it. I am afraid of getting too close, of getting too hurt, of being abandoned, of my heart being broken. That is what happens when you are a survivor of death, a child of tragedy, a son who has lost his immediate family too soon, a soul who can make sense of the world—all of the beauty and tragedy, grace and inhumanity—only by writing about it.

But I would not have been able to feel any of those emotions again if I hadn't given in to—over and over again—the rescues in my life. They taught me to live in the moment, to see the good in the world, to take a leap and love, and to be loved back unconditionally.

I needed them, it turns out, even more than they needed me.

We walked out with Cookie.

I held her in my lap the entire drive to his parents' home, while also holding my breath. When we arrived, Marge rushed into the house first. And then Cookie came charging in, running directly to Gary's father as if she knew exactly whom she needed to impress.

"Did you adopt another dog?" Gary's mom asked us.

"No," Gary said tentatively. "You did."

No one said a word. I was about to grab our gifts and run for the car, but Gary's father lowered himself onto the floor and began to play with Cookie.

"Who's a beautiful girl?" he called in singsong voice. "You are."

He looked up at us and smiled like a child who had gotten the bike he always dreamed of owning. Then, the man I'd never seen cry, teared up.

"She looks just like Midnight," he said, referring to the dog—another black Lab—the family had while Gary was growing up.

Cookie looked at him and licked his face, wagging her tail, the Christmas tree lights reflected in their eyes.

I never saw the two separated after that. They were like magnets. Cookie was calm, sweet, and seemed to understand Gary's father's limitations. Slowly, she brought him back to life. Gary's father began to walk Cookie, first around the yard, then the block, and then the neighborhood.

Gary's mom had something on which to dote—another grandchild—someone for whom she could make special treats and talk to while she was baking or gardening.

All fifty pounds of Cookie slept on Gary's dad's lap—in his beloved rocker—while they watched sports. And as his Parkinson's progressed, Cookie could always calm his trembling body.

When Cookie passed away this year—at nearly sixteen—we mourned her passing with many stories and even more tears.

For a decade and a half of holidays, Cookie was a part of their—and our—lives. She wore Santa hats. She opened gift bags, knowing a treat was waiting inside. She was, in short, the best Christmas present we ever could have gotten his parents.

This year, Gary's parents will get another dog. Not Cookie. There will never be another one like her, just like there will never be another Marge, who passed years ago, or Mabel and Doris, the two new dogs in—and who are the loves of—our lives.

But there will be a dog out there that brings them joy—and some pain—one they never knew existed. This dog may very well outlive Gary's father, who is now eighty-four. But this dog will likely add years of happiness to his parents' lives.

Sometimes, the wrong gift is right. Sometimes, the risk is worth it. Always, the love, I've learned, outweighs the pain.

It's just the way the cookie crumbles.

Alexander McCall Smith poses with an elephant on a trip to Botswana, the setting for his series The No. 1 Ladies' Detective Agency. *He visits the country every year.*

© CHRIS WATT

Baboons and Opera

ALEXANDER McCALL SMITH

I HAVE ALWAYS been interested in primates. We are primates ourselves, of course, and I suppose that for most of us, *Homo sapiens* is the most interesting sort of primate there is. But whatever fascination there may be in the study of human behaviour, there is something particularly intriguing about some of our hairier cousins—hence the discipline of primatology, one of the concerns of which is to illuminate behaviour that will seem strikingly similar to our own.

Some years ago, I was in northern Botswana in the Okavango Delta. This is a vast unspoilt region, home to numerous animals, from lumbering elephants to the tiny scurrying creatures of the undergrowth. I was there with my New York editor and agent, as I was keen to show them the country in which I had set my *No. 1 Ladies' Detective Agency* novels. We were in a boat, travelling along a river in the delta; on either riverbank were towering trees and fairly thick vegetation. As we rounded a bend in the river, I saw a small cluster of huts. Since it was a normally uninhabited area, I asked our guide who lived there. He replied that it was people who studied baboons, adding that the people did not like to be disturbed.

I suddenly realised that I knew exactly who they were. A few weeks earlier, I had read a rather specialized book entitled *Baboon Metaphysics*, a study of a troop of baboons in the Okavango Delta by two University of Pennsylvania primatologists, Dorothy Cheney and Robert Seyfarth. I prevailed upon our guide to take us over toward the camp, and as we approached the riverbank I cupped my hands and shouted, "I've just read *Baboon Metaphysics!*"

The effect was immediate. Out of one of the huts ran two primatologists, thrilled, I suspect, that somebody had read their dauntingly academic tome. They welcomed us ashore, and we had a cup of tea under the canopy of those towering trees. We talked about baboon social organization and, in particular, about how a female baboon might be ambitious for her mate. As this conversation was being conducted, the thought occurred to me that a female baboon might well be something of a Lady Macbeth. She was ambitious for her mate—which is putting it mildly.

I returned to Scotland. A few days later I had a meeting with Tom Cunningham, a composer with whom I have collaborated, as wordsmith, on numerous occasions. I suggested to Tom that I should write the libretto of an opera that told the story of *Macbeth* amongst a troop of baboons in the Okavango Delta. At first Tom wondered whether I was being serious, but then he came round to the idea. So we sat down and wrote an opera, *The Okavango Macbeth*, that deals with ambition and misdeeds in a troop of African baboons.

It was a ridiculous idea, but it worked. I had in the meantime set up a small theatre in the bush outside Gaborone, and we mounted the resulting opera there, not long after its completion. I attended the opening night, as did my New York agent, Robin Straus. It worked every bit as well as we had hoped it would. The singers were all local young singers who rarely had a chance to perform. One of them came up to me at the end of the evening and said, "This has been the best experience of my entire life."

I have often reflected on how that chance meeting brought about a most rewarding musical collaboration. Animals may bring people together, may inspire us in very different ways. Animals brought me to the writing of my first operatic libretto. That, in turn, resulted in singers coming together and getting all the enjoyment that is to be had from making music as a group. I am not sure what lesson is to be learned from all this, except possibly one that says that we are all joined together in this unpredictable, precious business of living, and that the animals are there too, mute perhaps, but members nonetheless of the same overall drama—whether it be opera, or anything else.

Lalita Tademy and her cat, Shadow, lived together for fourteen years, "two loners, fiercely independent, she and I."

Shadow

LALITA TADEMY

THERE ARE DOG people, and there are cat people. For the record, I am a die-hard cat person, despite the fact that I have proven to be pretty allergic to the aloof little creatures. Don't get me wrong. It's not that I can't appreciate the fierce loyalty that a dog bestows on its owner. But somehow, that particular brand of unwavering devotion feels vaguely unearned to me. What person in this world could possibly deserve that magnitude of allegiance all of the time, when fidelity is given no matter how badly the animal is treated?

Now, a cat, on the other hand, is pretty much in the game for itself. That's more my style. As a cat owner, you're constantly on probation. Take my adulthood pet, now in cat heaven for the last couple of decades. I'm assuming she made it to heaven, but I can't be sure. I named her Shadow, because from the time she was a tiny kitten she'd disappear for long stretches and then just turn up at my feet and follow me around unrelentingly demanding affection, with a full-throated purr you could hear in the next room. I got used to her absences as well as her love-ins. By the time I figured out I was allergic to her, it was too late. She and I were a team, and I just started taking shots to lessen the symptoms.

Shadow was an indoor cat, completely dependent on me for food and shelter, although she never seemed overly grateful. She was with me for fourteen years, during a time in my life when I was working long, exhausting hours climbing the corporate ladder in Silicon Valley.

I'd be gone on business trips for days at a time. She grew accustomed to my frequent three- or four-day absences, eating dry pellets from the seven-day cat feeder and drinking from the gravity water dispenser until I got back into town.

In the eighties, many promotions later, I started working for a Japanese company, and my international travel intensified. The trips got longer and more frequent. Only then did I discover that I couldn't board Shadow. Sweet as she could be with me, she could turn into a snarling, ferocious creature if anyone else tried to handle her. I truly didn't believe the first kennel when they refused to accept her for boarding a second time, but the next kennel I tried had the same experience. Hissing, aggressive, attacking behavior I'd never seen. After that, finally convinced, I'd have someone come to my house to look in on her every day for feeding and litter box duty, but mostly she'd hide from them until they were gone and she had the house to herself again. We were two loners, fiercely independent, she and I, demanding our own space, and coming together when it suited us.

Yes, she'd get in moods, as would I, but she was predictable. I'd come back from a trip and call out her name as soon as I passed through the front door. She would come running, make sure I saw her, and then turn her back to me and slowly walk away, tail in the air. Give her a little time, no more than an hour, and she'd pouted my abandonment away, and was ready to allow me back into her good graces.

At night, once the day was done, and I was bored, or happy, or lonely, or scared, or nervous, or excited, I'd call her name, and she would come and jump onto the foot of my bed. She'd respond every time, eventually, but only once she was ready, on her timetable. We coexisted well, mostly alone together. Sometimes together alone.

In her later years, Shadow got diabetes. I didn't know such a thing was possible. And so I found myself not only on the receiving end of weekly allergy shots but also administering two shots of insulin a day to my longtime pet. I changed her diet away from the ease of dry food to a special high-protein, low-carbohydrate moist mixture that took more care to prepare than some of my own meals. The old days of throw some dry pellets in a bowl and go on your way were over.

High maintenance was never what I had bargained for. And yet, in retrospect, I have to admit that Shadow gave me so much more than I could ever give her. Even now, all these years later, when I'm happily married and pet-less because of allergies, the memory of being able to call out to Shadow brings me a quiet comfort.

Shadow spent her last day on Earth in my arms as a vet administered the final relief for her pain. She trusted me. I cherished her. And upon careful reconsideration, I am absolutely certain she made it to cat heaven, on her own schedule.

Clifton Taulbert meets a new friend, Jack Sprat, and recalls his childhood in the Mississippi Delta.

JEREMY CHARLES

Peru and Saturday Afternoon Horses

CLIFTON TAULBERT

THIS STORY IS not about the "Grand Horses" for which the country of Peru is widely known, but the memories of a young black boy who grew up on the Mississippi Delta, where his social and economic life seemed to have been created in indelible ink, never to change. It was in his world of cotton and legal segregation that he was introduced to the "Grand Horses" of Peru Plantation, Mississippi.

I was that boy. When I was growing up in the late 1950s, the opportunity to ride horses on the Peru Plantation was one of my most memorable pastimes. In Glen Allan, where I was raised, my world seemed to have been socially and culturally set—and everything remained the same, except when venturing beyond Glen Allan to Peru Plantation, where our cousins lived and worked.

I was barely a teenager at the time, and for a Southern boy like me, riding a horse successfully could easily be called a coming-of-age activity. On those rare Saturdays with no work to be done, my parents would drive out to Peru to visit our cousins, of which there were many. Upon arriving at Peru's general store, the central place of plantation activity, I would be allowed to find my cousins and the children of the black overseers, who rode horses nearly every Saturday. And on some of those days, this group of young black boys would be integrated with the young white boys of the plantation owner.

It seemed as if all the boys from Peru, the black ones and the white ones, appeared to have no fear of those beasts. If you were standing close by their sides, they looked like giants on four legs, so it took me a while to pet and handle them, even as I watched the other boys. These were no small horses. These were the horses the men rode. I can still see myself being standoffish, that is until my big cousin Jimmy, much older than I, literally pushed me up to the side of the horse designated for my afternoon ride.

The other boys were handling their chosen steeds with great competence and seemingly no fear—feeding them lumps of sugar, brushing down their manes, and sometimes plaiting their long majestic tails. I was expected to do likewise, and I sheepishly did. My horse talked a bit in a language I didn't understand but one that seemed to agree that my brushing was just what he needed. In the corral where we had all gathered, the racial separation which had defined our world for generations took a backseat. The adults who had written the rules of legal segregation were absent, and the adults who had to follow them were absent as well. We were just boys and horses who had no social rules by which to abide.

Like those of us gathered in the corral, all the horses were different. I never thought about the diversity of the horses at the time, but was clearly aware of the gathering of the two races—a matter that didn't seem to count at all on those Saturday afternoons. In and around Peru's horse corral, a common ground had been established in the presence of those magnificent steeds.

Only first names were used. And my cousin Jimmy Lee knew them all. The white boys were young teenagers as well and no doubt had been schooled on the social restrictions to be observed, but none of this was discussed. Too much fun was in our future. On those Saturdays, it was all about riding the horses and going as fast as they would carry us.

In that setting, I was desperately trying to define myself as a big boy and a great rider. I could feel a spirit of competitiveness rising and quickly falling as I looked to my horse to understand all that was going on in my head. With all the horses rubbed down and brushed, we led them out of the barn and corral area to the open grounds, where it would be time to saddle up and ride with the wind. Jimmy was first to get on, followed by the other cousins and the two white boys, until finally it was my turn. I was scared on the inside, but dared myself to not show the fear. It took me several tries, but finally I was securely on my horse, just like the other boys. And off we went, nicely trotting along.

I was just fine. Sitting atop my steed with the sandy ground beneath me, I felt empowered. What a wonderful sense of accomplishment. These Saturday afternoon horseback rides were taking me out of the world that had relegated me to the rather routine life in the cotton fields of the delta.

The careful trotting that I could easily handle would soon turn to a much faster pace and flurries of dust, as the cowboys who were our collective heroes became our alter egos. We all wanted to be like them, the cowboys who came to town through the venue of the Dixie Theatre. I would sheepishly lean into the wind as the other boys did, becoming one with the ride. Being black, I had no hair to challenge the wind, but I could clearly feel the cool breeze finding the spaces in my own tightly curled hair—all throughout my scalp. As we passed the "shotgun" farmhouses, I tried to wave at folks sitting and talking on their front porches. It was hard to wave and hold on to the reins, but I tried. Finally we made it to the long "turn-road"—the makeshift race track for us—the road tractors used for turning when coming to the end of a row of work. It was the perfect place to race horses.

Even though I was excited, I wasn't as comfortable as the other guys, who rode almost daily and had been doing so all their lives. But I wasn't about to let them know my true feelings. I didn't have their confident swagger. I just leaned as low as I could against the broad neck of the horse and kept my eyes partially closed. I knew I would never be Roy Rogers. I was simply the cousin from Glen Allan, welcomed into this special world of Saturday afternoons, hosted by the Grand Horses of Peru Plantation.

Michael Wallis with Juniper (left) and Martini, his
feline companions and "beloved literary muses"

JOHN AMATUCCI

Touchstone

MICHAEL WALLIS

THANKS TO A seemingly delicate creature, I discovered that a sense of place is more than geography. My epiphany occurred many years ago, on an October morning filled with sunshine and promise.

My wife, Suzanne, and I drove to Sequoyah County in eastern Oklahoma to attend a Literary Landmark ceremony honoring Sequoyah, an illiterate Cherokee silversmith who created written language for his tribe by developing a syllabary in the late 1810s and early 1820s. The ceremony was being held ten miles northeast of Sallisaw—hometown of the fictional Joad family—at the one-room cabin that Sequoyah had built of hand-hewn logs in 1829.

En route, Suzanne and I talked about previous trips to the historic cabin and to the many other sites in the area we had often visited while I researched and wrote a biography of Charles Arthur "Pretty Boy" Floyd. The consummate Oklahoma bandit, Floyd is still remembered and often revered by the hardworking country folks who pass down stories about Pretty Boy like heirloom china.

As we drove southbound on the turnpike, a lone monarch butterfly flew into the windshield with a splat and became tangled in a windshield-wiper blade. We were saddened to see the beautiful butterfly end its short life in such a way. We knew that this was the precise time when the latest generation of summer monarchs made their journey thousands of miles southward from as far north as Canada to their wintering grounds. This was the time when they

flew over the landscape and danced across old Indian Territory just
as they had forever.

Some monarchs come to rest in the eucalyptus groves at
Pismo Beach and Big Sur in California. Others go even farther and
congregate by the millions on the south-facing slopes of the Sierra
Madres in Mexico, where they cloak the trunks of fir trees and
cluster in large masses on boughs to conserve heat. They rest all
winter. When they flex and flash their orange-and-black wings to
soak up the sun, the firs appear to be trimmed with jewels. In the
spring, when it is time to move northward again, the butterflies
cascade from the trees in a cloud bomb—waterfalls of sable
and saffron.

Our conversation turned back to memories of coming this
way with friends now gone and of other times, but each of us
could not help but see the monarch whose journey had ended
unceremoniously on the windshield. I knew Suzanne was especially
touched because she was at the wheel, which meant she felt she was
in some way culpable for the butterfly's death.

At Sallisaw we made a pit stop at a convenience store. While
I fetched waters, Suzanne got out of the car, carefully lifted the
wiper blade, and placed the crumpled monarch in her palm. I
took over as driver, and Suzanne said she wanted to make a stop
before we reached the event site. I knew in a heartbeat where she
wanted me to go.

Without a word being spoken, I turned off the highway and
into the Akins Cemetery. This quiet country graveyard was where
the largest funeral in state history took place on another October
morning, in 1934, when the slain Pretty Boy came home and
was laid to rest with other family members. We had visited the

graveyard many times, and it seemed familiar as we walked through formations of the dead marked by stones. We went directly to the Floyd family plot, where Pretty Boy lies next to his baby brother, E. W. Floyd, remembered as one of the best sheriffs ever in Oklahoma. As we stood there, Suzanne gently placed the monarch on Pretty Boy's granite tombstone. It was as if she were leaving a flower or remembrance for the outlaw who will be thirty years old forever.

As we stood there, the monarch inexplicably stirred and slowly lifted its wings. The wings seemed whole and caught the sunshine. Then suddenly the butterfly rose from the stone and fluttered above us before flying off to the south. Neither of us could speak. We just stood there with our mouths open and tears welling in our eyes. We watched the monarch until it was out of sight.

Then we went on the few short miles to the cabin where Cherokee tribal leaders, dignitaries, and citizens gathered to honor Sequoyah, a wise man who had made his own journey southward to Mexico and never returned. His bones are said to remain there in the warm sand. When I rose to speak during the ceremony, I told the story of the monarch. I felt compelled to share it. I saw many of the Cherokee people nodding, and some smiled. It seemed that they were not surprised by my simple story of resurrection.

Later, when I took time to consider the day, I understood the reaction. A Cherokee elder once told me that a butterfly brings special blessings when it passes over you. In some American Indian tribes, butterflies are thought to be the departed souls of ancestors. The emergence of the adult butterfly from a cocoon symbolizes the freedom of the soul. The butterfly metamorphosis is the greatest transformation in the animal world and stands as a symbol of new life, of change. The monarchs teach all of us that life is short and must be valued.

Like monarchs, some of the people of this land—Cherokees, Creeks, Choctaws, Chickasaws, and Seminoles—experienced long and arduous collective journeys. Like the fragile butterflies, they brought their sense of place with them on the various trails of tears they followed from their original homelands to what became Oklahoma. Through all the travails, they managed to keep a sense of place and bring it to their new home.

That is the truth of it. I know—because of a resilient butterfly in a country graveyard—that I carry my sense of place with me wherever I am.

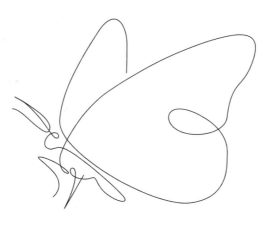

MARK BUTENHOFF

Mary Logan Wolf and Big Ted enjoy the sun in Cross Timbers country near her home in Luther, Oklahoma.

Bobcat Magic

MARY LOGAN WOLF

A S   A   Y O U N G girl not more than three or four, I liked to hover in front of the rumbling GE air conditioner wedged in the window of our family living room. The air conditioner mesmerized me: I thought lions lived there.

My mother found my notions amusing, if not a bit odd. I recall no conversations about my fixation, but once, she left a few trinkets there for me to find: small plastic lions tucked among the curtain drape atop the a/c. But my lions weren't caricatures. They were real, pacing the savanna of my imagination that for some reason existed just beyond the musty-smelling vents.

Funny how childhood fascinations prove prescient. I did not go on to become the Jane Goodall of lions or live a life à la *Born Free,* but I remain captivated by wildlife. Firmly planted in the red-dirt Cross Timbers of central Oklahoma, the acreage I share with my husband and three mutts is an uncultivated swath of post oak, hickory, and sand plum sliced in deep, canyon-like draws. It is a habitat well suited to my passions. Each day brings a tail feather, scrap of fur, or gnawed fragment of bone to serve as reminder of our cohabitant wild critters.

This morning, Big Ted roars out the back door on fire with canine purpose. With hackles stiff as a comb, he prances along the pond dam, nose in the air, throwing his barrel-chested warning into the timber. We've had visitors, Ted says, and he does not like their smell.

Later, I discover wild scat along the trail. Nearby, tracks from an animal traveling lithe and graceful. Notes from a bobcat. I've bushwhacked my share of backcountry, but until I moved here, glimpses of our native wildcat were all I had. A blur across the highway, a haunch disappearing into tall grass, a half-second tease that confirmed nothing. An almost sighting. For the feline that has called Oklahoma home for some 20,000 years, the bobcat manages to hide in the shadows with Yoko Ono–like secrecy. A good look at one is a four-leaf clover in the lapel of any animal lover. Three years ago, I hit the jackpot.

That morning I headed out for an aimless wander in the woods flanked by dogs of variable age and IQ. As I walked, they tramped through the forest duff with a familiar canine hyperbuzz, flipped on by the joy of wild smells. A few minutes passed, enough to lull me into a state of earth-induced bliss, when something hit me—no sounds. Worried, I scanned the woods and was relieved to spot the dogs just a few feet from the trail. But something was off. My once frenetic canine cabal sat stock-still beneath a tree, hyperbuzz now hyperfocused. I know my dogs. Such intensity is strictly reserved for the crème de la crème of doggie treats: the fat off a rib eye, the remains of last night's pot roast, a charred weenie dangling precariously off the end of a flimsy, whittled stick. Curious what would cast such a spell, I peered into the trees, half expecting to see a woodland giant bewitching my dogs with pork rinds. For me, it was something much better: *Lynx rufus.*

The bobcat stood poised on a branch not two feet beyond the reach of the tallest dog's nose. It stared down at the dogs, who stared up at the cat, while I stared at them all, locked as we were in an interspecies staring contest. Not a one of us blinked.

Realizing the *National Geographic* moment at hand, I fingered my pockets for the iPhone camera I had forgotten on the kitchen table. This was right before a rushing groundswell of adrenaline sent me pell-mell into what I now know to be a grade-A, celebrity-swooning senior moment.

First off, I was dumbstruck by the animal's size, over two tall feet tall and way larger than the tired-looking taxidermy specimens at Cabela's. Plainly, this was no run-of-the-mill feline. In the parlance of the county fair, this was a high-point winner, a hands-down blue-ribbon bobcat.

Since it was mammal and huge, I presumed it to be male. For the purpose of storytelling, "it" became "he"—and he was stunning, with thick fur in the muted tones of dried leaves and heavily peppered with dark spots. During Lewis and Clark's explorations of the Midwest, Native Americans presented them with exotic pelts. The explorers gave the skinned animal a name, which didn't stick, but as I gazed upon the creature, it struck me as entirely appropriate. *Behold, the tiger cat.*

In my post-bobcat mental processing, I realize I experienced an overwhelming compulsion to hold everything just so—*nobody move*—but of course I didn't. The slight shift of foot, a snap of twig, my heart pounding like a jackhammer; whatever, it was enough for the bobcat. He turned his head and looked squarely at me. My bobcat moment, eye-to-eye at fifteen yards. With his feral hoodoo trained on me, I found myself suddenly center stage in a bobcat improv. His ocher-colored orbs, carefully lined in ink, studied me with the regal intensity of an androgynous Ramses. Tufted ears tipped in black antenna-like hairs simply added to his otherworldly charisma. The bobbed tail, for which he is named, twitched slightly.

I suppose it is human nature to cling to the spectacular. In hindsight,

I'm ashamed to admit how I gripped that experience. I wanted to hold on to it, make it mine. Even in the retelling, I am aware of a stirring desire for a more tactile connection. Sadly, it's the marketing hook for every petting zoo from SeaWorld to Tiger Safari. In that human-centric way we allow our wants, curiosities, and fetishes to plow through the boundaries of other living beings, I wanted to touch the bobcat. I wanted to sink my fingers into its fur.

In the field of cultural anthropology, some theorize that up-close wildlife encounters precipitated the early deification of animals. Makes sense to me. If I were an artist, I would paint the bobcat. I would carve his totem. His likeness would become my petroglyph.

Call me anthropomorphic, but I'm pretty sure our wily grimalkin had different ideas. His eyes sizing me up, assessing the threat, every muscle fiber taut, his whole being hardwired by genetics to escape and survive. The bobcat embodied the antithesis of my human desires. Still, something in those wild, unblinking eyes spoke to me: *Soon I will disappear, and this moment is all you will have. Remember.*

One leap and a streak and he was gone.

Since my encounter, I've become keen on tracking. I'm an amateur at best, but it is the process I find most rewarding. My goal is not to find. I follow the signs: paw prints laid gracefully on the earth, flattened depressions in the leaves where something stopped to rest, the wilted feathers of a blue jay splayed across the forest floor in a haphazard haiku of death. I am learning the bobcat's wild system, the paths preferred, why this way and not that. It is a story I cannot stop reading.

Today, Big Ted tracks with me and tells me things. He stops near a draw where tangled greenbrier vines and fallen timber form a fortress. His nostrils shift slightly as some 300 million olfactory receptors process the incoming air. His ears, stuck permanently at half-mast, do their best to stand alert. He watches, nose twitching, keen on something just there. Kneeling beside him, I watch, too. A cold gust whips the breath from us and sends it rushing downwind, along with the scent of human and dog. A whir of wings as startled birds flush from the thicket beyond us, and somewhere the faint *shh-shh* of leaves shifting beneath the weight of something alive and moving, in the wild place.

Author and painter John Berger noted that we spend a lifetime looking at animals, but we rarely consider how animals see us. Once, I felt the bobcat watching me. It was early evening, following a brief but powerful Oklahoma tempest. I was drawn to the woods by the clean, fertile smell and the strange post-storm light that filtered through the leaves, giving every upturned blade a glinting edge. I trod lightly, careful to roll my weight gently heel to toe into the wet ground. Under the dripping canopy of jade, I felt like a solitary explorer in the Amazon, ever mindful of the potential of an incoming blow dart. As I made my way, I had the odd sense that something moved when I moved and stopped when I stopped.

If you've ever gotten a phone call at the time you're thinking about the caller, or stared at someone in a crowd who suddenly turns and looks at you, you've experienced the phenomenon of morphic resonance. The theory posits that all living things, from fungi to felines, maintain a collective memory that resonates within and around them. At times, we are maybe-possibly capable of sensing these vibrations. I believe skepticism is healthy, but at that moment I felt my internal psyche rattling like a gaggle of spooked geese. I was not alone in the woods—something was watching me. With a quick turn of a head, I caught the hint of a fur-bearing mammal slipping into the underbrush with distinct catlike stealth.

The bearers of good and bad mojo, bobcats weave their way through the ancient stories of Native Americans while providing ripe fodder for internet-based shamans who stalk the pages of Google. A bobcat is a message of caution, or a note to be patient, or a warning to look deeper into the motives of others, or a reminder to change the litter box. It's all mud in the water to me. I prefer to think of my bobcat encounter as a gift, a flash of something extraordinary, a doorway to a world we find increasingly rarely. I believe in bobcat magic, but it's a simple and gracious enchantment. It begins with a two-word incantation: Thank you.

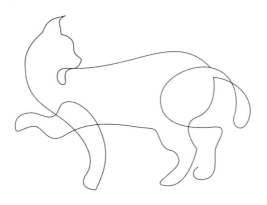

ABOUT THE AUTHORS

JULIA ALVAREZ is a novelist, a poet, an essayist, and a recipient of a 2013 National Medal of Arts. She has taught at the University of Illinois, the University of Vermont, and Middlebury College, where she also served as writer-in-residence. Among her published works are *Once Upon a Quinceañera, Where Do They Go?, Something to Declare, In the Time of the Butterflies*, and *How the García Girls Lost Their Accents*, which was selected by New York librarians as one of twenty-one classics for the twenty-first century. Her most recent collection of poetry is *The Woman I Kept to Myself*.

BLAKE BAILEY is the author of biographies of John Cheever, Richard Yates, and Charles Jackson, and he is working on the authorized biography of Philip Roth. He is the recipient of a Guggenheim Fellowship and an Award in Literature from the American Academy of Arts and Letters, the winner of the National Book Critics Circle Award and the Francis Parkman Prize, and a finalist for the Pulitzer Prize and James Tait Black Memorial Prize. His latest book, *The Splendid Things We Planned*, was a finalist for the National Book Critics Circle Award in Autobiography. He lives in Virginia with his wife and daughter.

RICK BASS began writing short stories on his lunch breaks while working as a petroleum geologist in Jackson, Mississippi. The Guggenheim Fellow's stories, articles, and essays have appeared in publications such as the *Paris Review, Harper's Magazine, Esquire*, and the *New Yorker*. His most recent works include *The Traveling Feast, Winter: Notes From Montana*, and a collection of stories, *For a Little While*, which won the Story Prize in 2017. The author and activist is chairman of the board of the Yaak Valley Forest Council, where he is engaged in land conservation and animal-protection efforts.

P. C. CAST is a No. 1 *New York Times* and *USA Today* best-selling author. A member of the Oklahoma Writers Hall of Fame, she is known for the blockbuster *House of Night* series she writes with her daughter, Kristin. This is in addition to her own Goddess Summoning novels and her new series, *Tales of a New World,* which features Cast's powerful connection with dogs. Cast has received a Holt Medallion and an Oklahoma Book Award. Two of her novels have been named YALSA Quick Picks for Reluctant Readers. In 2019, Cast and her daughter will launch another young-adult fantasy series, *The Dysasters.*

WAYNE COYNE is the front man for the Oklahoma City–based rock band the Flaming Lips. Visual artist, songwriter, musician, and creativity icon, Coyne has garnered a cult following since the band was formed in 1983. Coyne himself has collaborated with musical artists such as Miley Cyrus, the Chemical Brothers, and Mac DeMarco. The Flaming Lips' song "Do You Realize??" was named Oklahoma's State Rock Song in 2009. The Grammy Award winner is also a visual artist and the creator of the psychedelic fantasy comic book *The Sun Is Sick.*

KIM DONER was born in Tulsa, Oklahoma, where she helped organize the wildlife rehabilitation network WING-IT. Her work as an illustrator began in the medical field but has grown to encompass the illustration of her own children's books, including *Buffalo Dreams* and *On a Road in Africa,* based on her experiences at an animal orphanage in Kenya, where she worked with animal conservationists. Doner won the Oklahoma Book Award for her illustrations in *Green Snake Ceremony,* and she has collaborated with author P. C. Cast, crafting illustrations for *The Fledgling Handbook 101.*

DELIA EPHRON is a bestselling author, screenwriter, essayist, and playwright. She has written books of humor, books for children and young adults. Her most recent novels are *The Lion Is In* and *Siracusa*, which was chosen as one of *People* magazine's top-ten best books of 2016. Her movies include *You've Got Mail*, *The Sisterhood of the Traveling Pants*, *Michael*, and *Hanging Up* (based on her book). She and her sister, Nora Ephron, also cowrote the play *Love, Loss, and What I Wore*. "Dogs," the essay that appears in this collection, is from her memoir *Sister Mother Husband Dog (etc.)*.

REYNA GRANDE is an American Book Award–winning memoirist and novelist. In her memoir *The Distance Between Us*, a finalist for the National Book Critics Circle Award, Grande writes her story about life as an undocumented immigrant from Mexico. Other titles by Grande include *Dancing with Butterflies*, *Across a Hundred Mountains*, and her latest memoir, *A Dream Called Home*. In 2015, she received a Luis Leal Award for Distinction in Chicano and Latino literature. Additionally, Grande's books have been featured in common reading programs throughout the United States.

WOODY GUTHRIE carries on his legacy as an Oklahoma native through his continuing influence in American folk music. Guthrie's songs were often written with Oklahoma in mind, but he also remained inspired by the landscape of the country as a whole. After traveling from the East to the West Coast, Guthrie wrote his seminal song, "This Land Is Your Land." The title of this anthology is an excerpt from his commentary "My Secret": "Love can be and sure enough is moving in all things, in all places, in all forms of life at the same snap of your finger."

JOY HARJO, a member of the Mvskoke Nation, is a critically acclaimed poet, composer, musician, and performance artist. She is the author of eight collections of poetry, including *She Had Some Horses* and *Conflict Resolution for Holy Beings*, as well as the memoir *Crazy Brave*. A Guggenheim Fellow, Harjo has received many other honors, such as the Wallace Stevens Award from the American Academy of Poets and the Ruth Lilly Poetry Prize from the Poetry Foundation. Harjo also writes a column, "Comings and Goings," for her tribal newspaper, *Muscogee Nation News*.

AMY HEMPEL is the author of four collections of stories: *Reasons to Live, At the Gates of the Animal Kingdom, Tumble Home*, and *The Dog of the Marriage*. Her *Collected Stories* was named one of the *New York Times'* Ten Best Books of 2006. A Guggenheim Fellow, she has received many other awards, including the PEN/Malamud Award for Short Fiction. She is a founding board member of the Deja Foundation, a dog-rescue organization in New York City, and teaches in the Graduate Writing Seminars at Bennington College, and at Stony Brook Southampton.

JUAN FELIPE HERRERA was named California's poet laureate in 2012 and served two terms as US poet laureate—the first Mexican American to hold that honor. Herrera has published more than a dozen collections of poetry, including *Border-Crosser with a Lamborghini Dream*, and eleven young-adult and children's books, such as *Jabberwalking* and *Imagine*, an illustrated poem. A two-time recipient of Latino Hall of Fame Poetry Awards, Herrera taught in the creative writing department at the University of California, Riverside, until retiring in 2015.

S. E. HINTON is a Tulsa, Oklahoma, native with a long history of horseback riding. Hinton wrote the iconic young-adult novel *The Outsiders*, which was turned into the 1983 movie by the same title. Her unique young-adult style deemed her the "voice of the youth," and she became the first person to receive the Young Adult Services Division of the American Library Association and *School Library Journal* Author Achievement Award. Some of Hinton's other titles include *That Was Then, This Is Now*; *Rumble Fish*; and *Tex*—all of which became films. Most recently, Hinton published *Some of Tim's Stories*.

BRANDON HOBSON, an enrolled member of the Cherokee Nation, is an author of short stories, essays, and novels. His most recent novel, *Where the Dead Sit Talking*, garnered the attention of *Publishers Weekly*, receiving a starred box review. His other novels include *Desolation of Avenues Untold* and *Deep Ellum*. Hobson received a Pushcart Prize in 2016, and his writing has appeared in *Narrative Magazine*, *Conjunctions*, the *Paris Review Daily*, the *Believer*, and many other journals. He teaches in the language arts department at Northern Oklahoma College.

DEAN KOONTZ was a senior in college when he won an *Atlantic Monthly* fiction competition, which inspired him to pursue a writing career. In the years since, his books, widely and well reviewed, have sold over 500 million copies in thirty-eight different languages. He's one of only a dozen writers to have fourteen novels rise to No. 1 on the *New York Times* bestseller list, including *Sole Survivor*, *What the Night Knows*, and *The Bad Place*. His most recent titles are *The Forbidden Door* and *The Crooked Staircase*. Koontz has also written extensively about his late dog, Trixie.

URSULA K. LE GUIN was a celebrated and beloved author of twenty-one novels, eleven volumes of short stories, four collections of essays, twelve children's books, six volumes of poetry, and four of translation. The breadth and imagination of her work earned her five Nebula awards and five Hugo awards, along with a PEN/ Malamud Award and many other honors. In 2014 she was awarded the National Book Foundation Medal for Distinguished Contribution to American Letters, and in 2016 joined the short list of authors to be published in their lifetimes by the Library of America. Author Margaret Atwood remembers Le Guin as "always asking the same urgent question: What sort of world do you want to live in?"

JILL McCORKLE is the author of six novels, most recently *Life After Life*, and four story collections. Additionally her work, widely acclaimed, has appeared in numerous periodicals. Four of her short stories have been selected for *Best American Short Stories* and one essay, "Cuss Time," for *Best American Essays*. McCorkle has received many other honors, including the John Dos Passos Prize for Literature. Five of her books have been named *New York Times* notable books. She is currently a core faculty member in the Bennington Writing Seminars and frequently teaches at the Sewanee Writers Program.

LOUISA McCUNE is the executive director of Kirkpatrick Foundation in Oklahoma City, and cofounder and editor in chief of the contemporary art magazine, *ArtDesk*. For fourteen years she served as editor in chief of *Oklahoma Today*, and she has worked editorially with *Worth*, *George*, *Harper's Magazine*, and other magazines. She serves on the board of Animal Grantmakers and as an advisory trustee to Oklahoma Contemporary Arts Center and the Kirkpatrick Family Fund. McCune is a coeditor of this anthology and has written the introduction.

TERESA MILLER is coeditor of this anthology and director emerita of the Oklahoma Center for Poets and Writers at Oklahoma State University–Tulsa, where she taught creative writing. Her own books include *Remnants of Glory, Family Correspondence,* and *Means of Transit.* Miller was also executive producer and host of the television program *Writing Out Loud,* featuring in-depth interviews with leading writers. Additionally, she was founder and editor of the *Stories and Storyteller* series at the University of Oklahoma Press. Miller has been featured on C-SPAN and the *Diane Rehm Show.*

N. SCOTT MOMADAY, an enrolled member of the Kiowa Tribe, was born in Lawton, Oklahoma. Momaday grew up near the Navajo and San Carlos Apache communities. This intersection of culture informs his writing. Momaday's first novel, *House Made of Dawn,* won the Pulitzer Prize for fiction. A founding trustee of the National Museum of the American Indian, he has also published a collection of three plays, which tell the stories of his American Indian heritage. In 2007, he was awarded a National Medal of Arts. His latest collection of poetry, *Again the Far Morning,* includes nearly forty years of writing.

JOYCE CAROL OATES has written a number of works of prose, poetry, essays, and memoirs. Her most recent title is *Beautiful Days: Stories.* Additionally, she's the author of several children's books involving kittens and cats that are guaranteed to have purr-fectly happy endings. Some of those titles are *Naughty Cherie!* and, forthcoming in 2019, *The New Kitten.* A five-time Pulitzer finalist and a National Book Award winner, Oates has received numerous other distinctions, including the National Book Critics Circle Ivan Sandrof Lifetime Achievement Award. In 2010, President Obama presented Oates with a National Humanities

Medal. Also a publisher, Oates founded the *Ontario Review* with her husband in 1974. She teaches in Princeton University's creative writing program.

SUSAN ORLEAN is a staff writer for the *New Yorker,* and has also been a contributing writer for *Rolling Stone, Vogue,* and *Outside.* In 2004, Orlean was named a Neiman Fellow at Harvard University, and in 2012 she received an honorary doctorate of humane letters from the University of Michigan. She has served as a judge for the National Book Awards. Her 1998 book, *The Orchid Thief,* was the basis for the Academy Award– winning movie *Adaptation.* Her other books include *Rin Tin Tin: The Life and the Legend, The Floral Ghost,* and, most recently, *The Library Book.*

RON PADGETT is a poet, memoirist, essayist, translator, and chancellor emeritus of the Academy of American Poets. A Guggenheim Fellow, he has published more than twenty collections of poetry, including his *Collected Poems* and the Pulitzer Prize finalist *How Long.* As high school students, Padgett and his friends founded the *White Dove Review,* an art and literary journal that featured poets such as Allen Ginsberg and LeRoi Jones (Amiri Baraka). Seven of this native Tulsan's poems were used in Jim Jarmusch's film *Paterson.*

ELISE PASCHEN is a poet, an anthologist, a professor, and the daughter of Oklahoma prima ballerina Maria Tallchief. During her undergraduate studies at Harvard, she won the Lloyd McKim Garrison Medal, and later received her PhD in twentieth-century British and American literature from Oxford. A former executive director of the Poetry Society of America, she is a cofounder of Poetry in Motion, a nationwide program that places poetry posters in subway cars and buses. Her most recent titles include *The Nightlife*, *Bestiary*, and *Infidelities*, which won the Nicholas Roerich Poetry Prize.

DIANE REHM is a radio personality and voice of the *Diane Rehm Show*, which aired on National Public Radio for more than thirty years and garnered an on-air following of more than 2.8 million listeners. Known for her insightful interviews, Rehm has been included several times on *Washingtonian* magazine's "100 Most Powerful Women" list and is a recipient of a Personal Peabody Award and the National Humanities Medal. Among her published titles are *Finding My Voice*, *On My Own*, and *Life With Maxie*, about her beloved dog. Her podcast, *On My Mind*, features artists, writers, and thinkers, as well as Rehm's take on current issues.

JEWELL PARKER RHODES is a novelist, memoirist, and author of children's fiction, including *Towers Falling* and the *Louisiana Girls* trilogy. Rhodes first began writing stories inspired by the works of the other black writers she was reading. Some of her many honors include the American Book Award, the National Endowment of the Arts Award in Fiction, the Parents' Choice Award, the Jane Addams Children's Book Award, and the Coretta Scott King Author Honor Award. Her most recent novel, *Ghost Boys*, a *New York Times* best-seller, addresses "American blackness" and police brutality.

WADE ROUSE is the best-selling author of eight books, including *The Hope Chest* and *The Charm Bracelet*, both of which were written under Rouse's pen name, Viola Shipman, the name of his grandmother, whose family history inspires much of his writing. His latest Viola Shipman book, *The Recipe Box*, is the third in his "heirloom" series. His memoir *At Least in the City Someone Would*

Hear Me Scream was featured by NBC's *Today* show as a "Summer Must-Read." Rouse has also appeared on the National Public Radio show *All Things Considered* and written for numerous magazines, including *People* and *Coastal Living*.

ALEXANDER McCALL SMITH holds twelve honorary doctorates from American and European universities in addition to his earned doctorate and law degrees from the University of Edinburgh. He has received the Bollinger Everyman Wodehouse Prize for Comic Fiction, a Burke Medal, and most recently the Medal of Honor for Literature from the National Arts Club. Smith's *The No. 1 Ladies' Detective Agency* has garnered international attention as a best-selling series, alongside his recent titles *My Italian Bulldozer*, *The Sands of Shark Island*, and *A Time of Love and Tartan*.

LALITA TADEMY served as vice president and general manager of several Silicon Valley tech companies before settling into writing. The *New York Times* best-selling author has written three historical novels, including *Citizens Creek*, *Red River*, and *Cane River*, which was Oprah's Summer Book Pick in 2001. This debut work was translated into eleven languages and was assigned reading for all incoming freshmen at Stanford University in 2015. Tademy has appeared as a speaker for the Library of Congress, the National Book Festival, and the Professional Businesswomen of California.

CLIFTON TAULBERT is an author and entrepreneur, currently serving as president and CEO of the Freemount Corporation and Roots Java Coffee. *Eight Habits of the Heart*, one of his thirteen books, resulted in an invitation from former Supreme Court justice Sandra Day O'Connor to address members of the court. He has lectured at Harvard University Principals' Center and the United States Air Force Academy. Taulbert's books include Pulitzer Prize nominee *The Last Train North* and his debut work, *Once Upon a Time When We Were Colored*, which later became a major motion picture.

MICHAEL WALLIS is a historian and biographer of the American West, paying tribute to his travels in *Route 66: The Mother Road*. His award-winning reporting and writing can be found in nineteen books, including *Billy the Kid: The Endless Ride* and most recently *The Best Land Under Heaven*, an account of "the darkest side of Manifest Destiny." Wallis is a member of the Oklahoma Writer's Hall of Fame and is recognized internationally as a speaker and a voice talent. He can be heard as the sheriff of Radiator Springs in *Cars*, the animated Pixar film.

MARY LOGAN WOLF is a writer living in Luther, Oklahoma. Her works have been published in *Oklahoma Today* and *Oklahoma Living*. Her essay "Yes, Red State Liberals Exist" was recently featured in *Democracy: A Journal of Ideas* and on RealPolicy.com. Her poetry appears in *Ain't Gonna Be Treated This Way*, an anthology of protest and resistance poems honoring Woody Guthrie. When she isn't working, Wolf spends her time exploring the rugged Cross Timbers country near her home with her three dogs and, occasionally, her husband.

KIRKPATRICK FOUNDATION

Kirkpatrick Foundation is an Oklahoma City philanthropy that makes grants in the areas of arts, culture, education, animal wellbeing, environmental conservation, and historic preservation. The foundation was established in 1955 by John and Eleanor Kirkpatrick with an initial contribution of $10,000. In the years since, Kirkpatrick Foundation has given away more than $70 million in philanthropic funding. The foundation's approach to giving has been to maintain personal involvement with the charities and cultural activities of the community.

The foundation has played a key role in the development of many important Oklahoma City cultural institutions, including the Oklahoma City Museum of Art, Oklahoma Contemporary Arts Center, the Kirkpatrick Family Fund, the Oklahoma City Ballet, Science Museum Oklahoma, Lyric Theatre, the Oklahoma Zoological Society, and the Joan Kirkpatrick Animal Hospital at the Oklahoma City Zoo.

In 2012, the foundation commenced a major initiative to make Oklahoma the safest and most humane place to be an animal by the year 2032, working with stakeholders, nonprofits, the private sector, government agencies, and individuals on the front lines of animal wellbeing in the areas of companion animals, farm animals, wildlife, exotics, equine, laboratory animals, pollinators, and the human-animal bond.

HONORARIA

Kirkpatrick Foundation donated these authors' honoraria to the non-profit animal charities of their choice. The remaining authors made private gifts.

P. C. Cast: Humane Society of Tulsa, Tulsa, Oklahoma

Wayne Coyne: Bella Foundation SPCA, Oklahoma City, Oklahoma

Kim Doner: WING-IT, part of the Tulsa Audubon Society, Tulsa, Oklahoma

Delia Ephron: Ghetto Rescue Foundation, Los Angeles, California

The Estate of Woody Guthrie: Oklahoma Westie Rescue, Bixby, Oklahoma

Joy Harjo: Native America Humane Society, Torrance, California

Amy Hempel: Deja Foundation, New York, New York

Juan Felipe Herrera: Central Valley SPCA, Fresno, California

S. E. Hinton: Street Cats, Tulsa, Oklahoma

Brandon Hobson: Ponca City Humane Society, Ponca City, Oklahoma

Dean Koontz: Canine Companions for Independence, Oceanside, California

Jill McCorkle: Buddy Dog Humane Society, Sudbury, Massachusetts

Teresa Miller: Enid SPCA, Enid, Oklahoma

Joyce Carol Oates: Small Animal Veterinary Endowment, Skillman, New Jersey

Susan Orlean: American Fondouk Maintenance Committee,
     Boston, Massachusetts

Elise Paschen: Native America Humane Society, Torrance, California

Diane Rehm: Tulsa SPCA, Tulsa, Oklahoma

Wade Rouse: 4 Paws Lakeshore, Douglas, Michigan

Michael Wallis: Save Our Monarchs, Minneapolis, Minnesota

Mary Logan Wolf: Peaceful Animal Adoption Shelter, Vinita, Oklahoma

BENEFICIARIES

The following nonprofit organizations will receive all net proceeds from this book, divided equally among them.

BELLA FOUNDATION

Bella Foundation SPCA is a foster-based rescue in Oklahoma City. Bella provides veterinary assistance to low-income, elderly, and terminally ill pet owners and assists in finding permanent homes for rescued animals. Its foster program provides temporary shelter until animals are formally adopted. Animals receive individualized care in a home setting, giving them better socialization skills and allowing for an accurate assessment of personality, temperament, and behavioral traits. Bella rescues will stay in foster care for as long as it takes to find them the right home. Bella provides for all needs of rescued pets, along with twenty-four-hour support for foster homes. Every foster animal is spayed or neutered, vaccinated, microchipped, tested for heartworm, and given basic training.

ENID SOCIETY FOR THE PREVENTION OF CRUELTY TO ANIMALS

Enid SPCA, in Enid, Oklahoma, offers a range of programs, including adoptions, spay-neuter assistance, and pet food for owners in financial need. Enid SPCA is a live-release shelter, and its hard work through Rescue Waggin', a partnership with a network of other shelters and Enid Animal Control, places animals into loving homes throughout the United States. The fostering program provides support for those volunteer homes, assisting them with medical care (including vaccinations, spaying and neutering, and microchipping), kennels, food, and an online network of other animal foster homes and volunteers. This program allows the Enid SPCA to save animals even when the kennels are full.

JOAN KIRKPATRICK ANIMAL HOSPITAL

The Joan Kirkpatrick Animal Hospital is located on the grounds of the Oklahoma City Zoo and was completed in 2015, with a significant gift from the Kirkpatrick Foundation and Kirkpatrick Family Fund and support from the community at large. The 20,000-square-foot facility provides expert veterinary services for more than 1,900 animals at the zoo, which is Oklahoma's premier destination connecting people and the world's wildlife. The facility offers the opportunity to view medical procedures from an observation window above the examination area. Bolstering conservation efforts, this state-of-the-art hospital benefits fifty-four endangered or threatened species. The Oklahoma Zoological Society is the supporting nonprofit organization for the zoo.

WILDLIFE IN NEED GROUP-IN TULSA

WING-IT is a network of volunteer rehabilitators under the umbrella of the Tulsa Audubon Society in Tulsa, Oklahoma. The group is dedicated to the rehabilitation of orphaned, sick, injured, or otherwise displaced native wildlife, with the goal of releasing them back into the wild. Rehabilitation specialists assist and support efforts to save wildlife and educate the public regarding the care of wildlife in need. The Tulsa Audubon Society promotes the conservation of wildlife and the natural environment and provides opportunities to study and observe birds and wildlife. The organization also contributes to conservation and ornithology research and educates the public on the need to protect the environment.

TULSA SOCIETY FOR THE PREVENTION OF CRUELTY TO ANIMALS

Tulsa SPCA provides adoption services, vaccinations, microchipping, and spay and neuter surgeries through a low-cost veterinary clinic. Its Mobile Adoption Center (MAC) regularly travels to events, public parks, and retail areas to promote onsite adoptions. The organization also arranges educational presentations for elementary and middle schools, and provides companion animals for patients at nursing homes and other extended-care facilities. Especially committed to its overall mission of "preventing cruelty to animals," Tulsa SPCA keeps a trained cruelty investigator on staff, working in association with Tulsa Animal Welfare and law enforcement.

WILDCARE FOUNDATION

WildCare Foundation provides people with a place to bring injured or ailing wildlife—perhaps accident victims or those orphaned too young to make it on their own. Its facility in Noble, Oklahoma, serves as a temporary residence for more than 140 species and includes 13,400 square feet of enclosures for mammals and 26,100 square feet of outdoor aviaries on seven acres. WildCare is licensed by the Oklahoma Department of Wildlife Conservation and the US Fish and Wildlife Service, permitting the foundation to work with migratory birds, including bald and golden eagles. WildCare is aided by animal-care students from various states, university work-study students, other volunteers, and a compassionate public bringing animals in need to the facility.

ACKNOWLEDGMENTS

Creating an anthology with thirty distinguished authors, thirty photographers, two editors, a team of publishing experts, and a menagerie of animals is a surprisingly complex task.

Many thanks are in order.

First, to the many wonderful writers, "from California to the New York island; from the Redwood Forest, to the gulf stream waters" (to quote Woody Guthrie once again), who so willingly shared with us their talents in eighteen original pieces and twelve reprints.

Our thanks to Christian Keesee, chairman of the Kirkpatrick Foundation and the son of Joan Kirkpatrick—to whom this book is dedicated—for his enduring support of these creative endeavors, and to each of the trustees of Kirkpatrick Foundation, former and current from the beginning of this project: Robert Clements (president), Rebecca McCubbin (vice president), Louisa McCune (secretary), Max Weitzenhoffer (treasurer), George Back, Elizabeth Farabee, Mischa Gorkuscha, David Griffin, George Records, Mark Robertson, Glenna Tanenbaum, and advisory trustee Elizabeth Eickman.

Much gratitude to Alana Salisbury, the managing editor for the book, who added this project to her busy schedule and facilitated the details with grace; Kathy McCord, office manager of Kirkpatrick Foundation, for her administrative support; Jim Cholakis, a supreme copy editor; and Kelly Rogers, for her editorial and fact-checking support.

For design, we thank designer Christopher Lee, whose patience and talent served the book each step of the way, and Steven Walker, for his generous input; illustrator JJ Ritchey, for her animal line drawings;

and book-packaging expert Emmy Ezzell, who guided the way on manufacturing. Thanks also to Dale Bennie of the University of Oklahoma Press, for overseeing the distribution of the book.

Thank you to the thirty photographers whose work—from snapshots to studio portraiture—is featured in these pages, and to our cover photographer, Joel Sartore, whose career documenting the world's animals captures the intent of *Love Can Be*.

Additional thanks to Theo Downes-Le Guin, Ginger Clark, Robin Straus, Stuart Bernstein, Will Kaufman, Tanya Farrell, Frank Graham, John Drayton, Jo Ann Reece, Jill Momaday, Kristi and Jack Morris, Judy Hubble, Lorraine Walker, Karen Kircher, and the entire staff of Kirkpatrick Foundation, all of whom contributed to the making of this special book.

Last but never least, we thank the dear, funny, peculiar, old, and young animals in our lives, who provided steady companionship throughout—they are the heart and soul and inspiration for this book. Roxy, Libby, Scout, Carl, Suzy, Cormac, Rocka Grey, Benny, Holland, Ollie, Gus, Duke, Mr. B, Ted, and so many more in spirit whose lives and legacies live on in these pages.

COPYRIGHTS AND SPECIAL PERMISSIONS

The editors wish to express their deepest gratitude to the publishers and writers who granted us special permission to print select pieces.

"Animals and Art" is used by permission from *Collected Poems* (Coffee House Press, 2013). Copyright © 2013 by Ron Padgett.

"Baboons and Opera," by Alexander McCall Smith, copyright © 2018 by Alexander McCall Smith. Used by permission of Alexander McCall Smith and his literary agent, Robin Straus Agency, Inc. All rights reserved.

"The Bear" from *In the Presence of the Sun: Stories and Poems, 1961–1991* by N. Scott Momaday, copyright © 2009 by N. Scott Momaday. Used by permission of University of New Mexico Press.

"The Cat," by Ursula K. Le Guin, copyright © 2018 by the Estate of Ursula K. Le Guin. Used by permission of the Estate of Ursula K. Le Guin.

"Dog Memory," by Susan Orlean, copyright © 2010 by Susan Orlean. Originally published in *Culture Desk,* the *New Yorker* (www.newyorker.com), August 4, 2010. Used by permission of the *New Yorker*/Condé Nast.

"Dogs," from *Sister Husband Mother Dog (etc.)* by Delia Ephron, copyright © 2013 by Delia Ephron. Used by permission of Blue Rider Press, an imprint of Penguin Publishing Group, a division of Penguin Random House LLC. All rights reserved.

"In Honor of Mo Who Is Our Cat, and We Are Hers," by Joy Harjo, copyright © 2002 by Mekko Productions, Inc. Used by permission of Mekko Productions, Inc.

"JUBILATE: An Homage in Catterel* Verse," by Joyce Carol Oates, copyright © 2015 by *Ontario Review*, Inc. Originally published in the *New Yorker*, July 28, 2015. Used by permission of *Ontario Review*, Inc.

"Moonbow" by Amy Hempel, copyright © 2007 by Amy Hempel. Originally published in the *American Scholar*. Used by permission of Amy Hempel.

"Naming the Animals" and "The Animals Review Pictures of a Vanished Race" from *The Woman I Kept to Myself*. Copyright © 2004 by Julia Alvarez. Published by Algonquin Books of Chapel Hill in 2004. By permission of Susan Bergholz Literary Services, New York, NY, and Lamy, NM. All rights reserved.

"Prey" from *Bestiary* by Elise Paschen, copyright © 2009 by Elise Paschen. Used by permission of Red Hen Press.

"Redbird Love" by Joy Harjo, copyright © 2017 by Mekko Productions, Inc. Originally published by *Poetry* magazine. Used by permission of Mekko Productions, Inc.

"A Spooky Moment Around Which the Entire Story Revolves," from *A Big Little Life* by Dean Koontz, copyright © 2009 by Dean Koontz. Used by permission of Bantam Books, an imprint of Random House, a division of Penguin Random House LLC. All rights reserved.

Excerpt from "My Secret" © Woody Guthrie Publications, Inc. Used by permission.

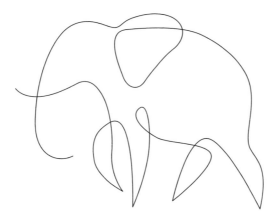

THE TYPE

The typefaces used in *Love Can Be: A Literary Collection About Our Animals* are Dante, Fournier, and Brandon Grotesque.

Designed by Giovanni Mardersteig in Italy shortly after World War II, Dante is a beautiful typeface, ideal for books and magazines. Used in *Love Can Be* as the body text, it was created at Mardersteig's hand-press facility, the Officina Bodoni. The face was formally adapted by Monotype in 1957 and updated by Ron Carpenter in 1993.

Fournier is another serif typeface used in *Love Can Be*, originally designed in the mid-1700s by Pierre-Simon Fournier and re-released in 1924. This headline face is recognized for its formal French elegance and ornamental style and is considered a bridge between Old Style and Modern serif designs. Fournier was well known in his era as a typographic theoretician.

Lastly, Brandon Grotesque is a sans-serif typeface designed by Hannes von Döhren of HvD Fonts in 2009 and 2010. Döhren lives in Berlin and continues to design typefaces at his German foundry for companies as varied as Lufthansa, Volkswagen, and Walmart. Brandon Grotesque is much like Helvetica, in that it is considered one of the most successful typefaces in modern times.